Augsburg College
George Sverdrup Library
Minneapolis, Minnesota 55404

CURRENT PEACE RESEARCH
AND INDIA

CURRENT PEACE RESEARCH AND INDIA

MAHENDRA KUMAR, *Ph. D.*
Department of International Politics and Organization
Indian School of International Studies, New Delhi

GANDHIAN INSTITUTE OF STUDIES
Rajghat, Varanasi, India

PRICE : RUPEES EIGHTEEN ONLY

© GANDHIAN INSTITUTE OF STUDIES, 1968

PUBLISHED BY SUGATA DASGUPTA FOR THE GANDHIAN INSTITUTE OF STUDIES, RAJGHAT, VARANASI, AND PRINTED AT INDRAPRASTHA PRESS (CBT), NEW DELHI.

Foreword

Peace research as a specialized and distinct research activity is a comparatively new development in social science research. But in the sense Gunnar Myrdal has used the term, namely that it is a systematic study in the diverse fields of social science as a result of which our understanding of conflicts, tensions, or wars improves, peace research is as old as social science research itself. Yet I cannot agree with Myrdal's further observation that not much purpose is served by delineating (for peace research) a specific area of its own. Because, unless a deliberate and pointed attempt is made to develop research in problems of peace and war and of violence in general, there will be no likelihood of this vital branch of research receiving the kind of attention which it deserves and which is also the urgent need of the hour. For proof one has only to compare the unsurpassed importance of the question of peace with the meagre output of peace research *prior* to the time when it began to be developed as a distinct branch of research. That development has not only served to focus attention on the need for peace research but also contributed to the growth of a valuable amount of knowledge on the subject. It is, of course, possible to be sceptical about the value of research for the task of peace-making, but that would be to doubt the efficacy of human reason and the scientific method.

In our country, in spite of the great nonviolent movement led by Mahatma Gandhi and the long historical tradition of *shanti* and *ahimsa,* practically no work has so far been done in the field of peace research. There is, of course, a considerable and very valuable ancient literature on the subject of man's inner peace: its nature and the discipline necessary to acquire it. That literature is no doubt the product of scientific enquiry and experimentation. But the ancients gave little thought to the problems of war and other forms of social violence.

Since India became independent, there have been several external aggressions, continued tensions on the frontiers, and internal violence of diverse kinds. Even the ancient science of inner personal peace has survived more as something to boast about than as a guide to practical life. So there is today neither internal nor external peace in our country. In this situation, it is a matter of much regret that social science research in this country has so far nearly completely neglected the field of peace research. Except for the study of the Rourkela riots by Dr B.B. Chatterjee and his colleagues at the Gandhian Institute of Studies, I know of no serious work of research in this field.

Guided by these thoughts, I took the opportunity in my Convocation address to the University of Mysore in November 1965 to draw the attention of the universities and research institutions in India towards the urgent need for taking up systematic research in problems of peace. Later, the Gandhian Institute took up this question and as a first step decided to have a competent researcher prepare a preliminary survey of peace research work done hitherto in India and abroad. We were fortunate in persuading Dr Mahendra Kumar of the Indian School of International Studies to accept this assignment for us. The result of his labours is being presented in this volume. The first part of this monograph, entitled "The Present State of Peace Research", makes an attempt to discuss the scope of peace research, its aims, and its potentialities as a science. The second part deals with the broad areas in which peace research can and should be conducted in India. The third part of the monograph attempts a critical evaluation of about 150 publications in the field of peace research. This evaluation indicates, on the one hand, the present trends in peace research and, on the other, the gaps that can be filled by peace researchers in this country or abroad. The last section contains a list of important research centres in various parts of the world that are engaged in peace research directly or indirectly.

I hope this able monograph will be found useful not only by all scholars and research institutions interested in this new and vital branch of scientific enquiry but also by all peace workers in this country.

Patna
5 January 1968   JAYAPRAKASH NARAYAN

Preface

In no other period of history has man been so much concerned with the problem of peace as he is today. This is so not only because of the all-destructive character of modern war but also because of the growing conviction that all sections of humanity are capable of contributing to the cause of peace. One of these sections of humanity, namely the scholars, believes that an important way to solve the problem of peace is to identify causes of war and conditions of peace in various areas of human relationships. This belief has led to the development of the science of peace research which can be described as the intellectual effort to produce knowledge about the phenomenon of violence and suggest measures for its control. Peace research has thus brought about a kind of revolution in social science research during the last ten years or so. Unfortunately, however, this revolution has not attracted the attention of scholars in India so far, so much so that there is hardly any awareness in this country of this fast-developing discipline of peace research. But, as peace research can grow only after a certain level has been achieved in international relations research and since research in this field in India has not yet achieved maturity, this lack of awareness is not surprising.

Nevertheless, it was indeed very satisfying that the Gandhian Institute of Studies, especially its Honorary Director, Mr Jayaprakash Narayan, and its Joint Director, Professor Sugata Dasgupta, should have thought of taking steps to create an awareness in India of this new science of peace research and to start a peace research programme in this country. As a first step, the Gandhian Institute decided to hold, with the collaboration of the Institute of Social Sciences,

Agra, an international conference on peace research (to be held at Varanasi from 18 to 20 January 1968). This book has been written specially for this conference. I am grateful to Mr Jayaprakash Narayan and Professor Sugata Dasgupta for inviting me to prepare this book and for offering me the facilities needed for its completion.

Yet it would not have been possible for me to complete the book without the kind permission of the Director of the Indian School of International Studies, New Delhi, to include here my survey article entitled "Recent Studies in Peace Research" which was originally planned for publication in *International Studies,* the quarterly journal of the School. I also thank my colleague, Mr. M.L. Sondhi, M.P., who was initially responsible in his capacity as Head of the Department of International Politics and Organization at the School for my preparation of the survey article and who has been encouraging me to do more extensive work in the field of peace research. I must specially acknowledge the ready help given by my esteemed friend, Mr A.S. Hebbar, by way of his skilful editing of the manuscript. Thanks are also due to Mr Girja Kumar, Librarian of the School, for his help in the search for material; and to my wife, Mrs Kusum Agrawal, for her assistance in preparing the press copy and correcting the proofs.

New Delhi
8 January 1968   MAHENDRA KUMAR

CONTENTS

The Present State of Peace Research	1
Possibilities of Peace Research in India	33
Recent Studies in Peace Research	62
Appendices	127
Index	143

CHAPTER ONE

The Present State of Peace Research

In a conference on peace research held at Clarens, Switzerland, in 1963, several members raised the question "what is peace research?", and the only conclusion that could be arrived at was that the simplest definition would be that peace research is whatever one is doing with the conviction that he is carrying on peace research.[1] This broad definition is appropriate in one respect and inappropriate in another. It is appropriate because it covers all men as capable of contributing to peace with which all men are obviously concerned. But it is inappropriate because the concept of "whatever one does with the conviction that he is carrying on peace research" is vague. The words "whatever one does" can be interpreted in simple terms to mean "every activity". But research is not any kind of activity. It is a very special kind of activity. The conviction of carrying on peace research is also vague unless one is aware of what is meant by peace research. Thus the definition of peace research adopted at Clarens is inadequate. Its only merit lies in its indirect reference to the fact that peace research has much too wide a scope to be defined or identified.

I

But defining and identifying the scope of an area of study is what precisely is the function of scholars. Those working in the field of peace research have attempted to perform this function, though there is hardly any definite agreement among them on the meaning of peace research except at a very high level of generality with regard to the objective of peace research. This objective may be stated as the achievement of peace; and

[1] See *International Newsletter on Peace Research* (Ann Arbor), Vol. 1, No. 3, p. 3.

research conducted for the realization of this objective is peace research. In other words, research for peace[2] is peace research. Outside a very broad agreement on the achievement of peace as the objective of peace research, there is little unanimity of opinion about the content of peace research. One reason for the lack of this unanimity is the fact that peace research as an independent area of study is still in the process of evolution. The other reason is that the meanings given to the expressions "peace" and "research" are often varied. Consequently the meaning of "peace research" should also vary.

It is obvious, therefore, that any attempt to define peace research would be fruitless unless preceded by an attempt to define "peace" and "research". The term "peace" does not convey a definitively intelligible idea. It may conceal objectives which are opposed to each other. Different people may give different interpretations to it and accordingly may follow different policies which may frustrate the realization of any kind of peace. The supporters of *status quo*, for example, may defend their position on the plea for considerations of peace but this may frustrate progress towards justice. On the other hand, the attempt to realize justice may pose a threat to order and stability or, in other words, peace. There may also be a confusion between peace in the abstract and peace in the concrete. The former implies a permanent condition of peace throughout the world for all time, whereas the latter refers to an actual situation in the relationship between two or more nations marked by the termination of hostilities or the relaxation of tensions. The first purpose of the United Nations is to "maintain international peace and security" and the purpose of the Unesco is to "contribute to peace and security by promoting collaboration among the nations through education, science, and culture". The Quakers and various other peace sects have persisted in their attitude towards peace and have proposed practical policies to prevent war.[3] The suggestions

[2] The Institute for Social Research, Oslo, organized a prize contest on the relevance of scientific research to the peaceful solution of international conflicts. The three prize-winning essays were published in a book form under the title *Research for Peace Essays* (Amsterdam, 1954).

[3] For details of the ideas of various peace sects see C.M. Case, *Non-violent Coercion: A Study in Methods of Social Pressure* (London, 1923); Frank M. Russell, *Theories of International Relations* (New York, 1936); and Elfrida Vipont, *The Story of Quakerism Through Three Centuries* (London, 1960).

for these policies are based on various arguments, religious, economic, ethical, and moral. Yet it is difficult to deduce any generally accepted definition of peace from them. The whole history of peace movements also fails to provide any such definition of peace. On the other hand, the term "research" is also susceptible to various meanings. In academic circles the term evokes the image of a dedicated and dispassionate endeavour to discover truth. If this concept of research is used in trying to define peace research, a number of difficulties come up. For one thing, the history of man has had very few, brief periods which can be called peaceful. Secondly, a dedicated and dispassionate search is undertaken for the sake of the discovery of truth itself, which is not the only objective of peace research. As stated earlier, the objective of peace research is the achievement of peace irrespective of whatever one may understand by peace.

The above remarks would show that those who demand peace do not have the same conception of it and that the concept of purely academic research does not exhaust the whole area of research needed for peace. Modern technology has created conditions in which research is considered a panacea for every difficult problem. As such, any scholarly activity aimed at seeking solution to a problem is called research.[4] Research in this sense is applied research. It can be applied to any attempt to utilize rational thought and available data in finding a solution to a reasonably well-defined problem. In the context of present discussion, the problem is clearly the avoidance of war and the maintenance of peace. A partial definition of peace research can, therefore, be that it is an attempt to find out ways and means for the solution of the problem of war and peace. Here the question of war also enters into the scope of peace research. Actually it would not be far from truth to say that the whole interest in peace research has grown as a reaction against the ever-increasing destructiveness of war. Peace research is thus an answer to

---

[4] See Wilson Gee, *Social Science Research Methods* (New York, 1950); Ernest Nagel, *The Structure of Science* (London, 1961); Charter V. Good and Douglas E. Scates, *Methods of Research* (New York, 1954); Max Weber, *The Methodology of the Social Science* (New York, 1949); and British Academy, *Research in the Humanities and the Social Sciences* (London, 1961).

what Norman Alcock calls a felt need to eliminate war[5] and, consequently, to achieve peace. This need, however, is not clearly articulated. For if the realization of the need for peace were as general as it appears and if all had the same conception of peace, then perhaps peace could be established. But since this is not so, it means that the problem of peace is not correctly understood. The first task of peace research, therefore, is to define the problem of peace and achieve a consensus on a definition which is neither vague nor self-contradictory. Research is needed for enriching the human understanding of the problem of peace. Having defined the problem of peace, peace research takes up the problem of determining the extent to which one can establish criteria for the delimitation of research of direct relevance to the problem of peace. In trying to deal with these two problems, peace research is not only suggesting ways for the elimination of war but also contributing to the conceptual growth of "peace" and "research". Let it be added, however, that the contribution being made by peace research at the present stage of its development is clearer and more definitive in the case of "research" than it is in the case of "peace". For while there is substantial unanimity among peace researchers on their answer to the question as to what is research, there is no such clear unanimity on the question as to what is peace.

Two relevant questions arise here. One is concerned with the peculiarity of the concept of research applicable to the problem of peace and the other with the nature of the difference of opinion among peace researchers on the question of the meaning of peace.

The peculiarity of the concept of research in the context of peace research lies in the emphasis that research has two sides: pure and applied. Earlier it was stated that pure research alone is inadequate and that applied research is of great significance for peace. But applied research divorced from pure research is as inadequate as pure research divorced from applied research. Pure research which is concerned with the discovery of truth for its own sake is indeed significant, but it is useless unless applied to man's need. Academic

---

[5] Norman Z. Alcock, "The Meaning and Purpose of Peace Research", *Gandhi Marg* (New Delhi), Vol. 35, July 1965, p. 206.

research in demography, for example, is concerned with population densities in various parts of the world. But applied research on the population problem covers a wide range of activities including development of contraceptives and finding new sources of food. Demography and the population problem are thus interrelated. The same is the case with the interrelationship between academic research and applied research in the context of peace. Pure research discovers causes of war and conditions of peace, whereas applied research seeks to find out ways in which causes of war may be averted and conditions of peace may be created. Pure research seeks knowledge and applied research utilizes that knowledge for the satisfaction of human needs. What necessitates this equation between pure research and applied research is the realization of the existence of a problem. Thus the problem of peace is to peace research what the problem of population is to demography. It is the insistence of making knowledge available for the solution of a problem that imparts a peculiar character to the meaning of research in peace research. This peculiar character consists in the emphasis on the problem-knowledge equation. In other words, research has to be problem-oriented. It has to proceed with an objective of acquiring knowledge with a view to using it for the solution of the practical problems of man. The acquisition of knowledge is incidental, though not unimportant. The link between peace and research, therefore, is a link between problem and knowledge. Peace research seeks to establish this link and give purposiveness to both knowledge and research.

This brings us to the second question, namely the nature of the purpose for which knowledge acquired through pure research has to be utilized. It is in the realm of defining this purpose clearly that efforts have been less successful. Although in one word this purpose may be described as peace, difficulties arise when one comes to details. Peace is generally regarded as the antithesis of war. But it is also taken as "the conclusion of warlike operations" or the "absence of war". After the Second World War greater emphasis has been laid on peaceful settlement of international problems. More recently, expressions like "peace-keeping" have come into vogue. Under the impact of the advent of nuclear weapons, writers like Leo Hamon[6] and Jules Moch[7] now understand peace in terms of warlessness. Although in a generic sense the term "warlessness" refers to a hypothetical world situation in which disarmament has been achieved, decisions of the International Court of Justice are enforceable, an international police force has been established effectively, and the veto has been abolished in the Security Council, yet the term is often used to describe the continuance of the present situation characterized by the absence of a major war. In this sense warlessness simply means the indefinite postponement of a nuclear war. Thus the term "peace" has no widely accepted connotation.

But the lack of an agreed connotation is due to numerous difficulties involved in making the world suddenly peaceable. Although the ultimate objective is the elimination of war, the achievement of this objective is possible only through stages. These stages may be called the short-term objectives, as against the long-term or ultimate objective, which is the elimination of war. The long-term objective belongs to the realm of the desirable and the short-term objectives belong to the realm of the possible. The difference of opinion is not so much about what is desirable as about what is possible. For the elimination of war is admittedly the desirable end. But since the attainment of the desirable does not seem possible in the immediate future, an attempt to achieve the possible is the only alternative.

However, any attempt to achieve the possible is itself a part of a larger problem, namely the development of a stable high-level world society. The development of such a world society involves a major intellectual task of discovering the knowledge on which the world society can be based and which could provide effective means of conflict management, which could give guidelines for economic development and population control, and which could help in a sane development of material technology. Kenneth Boulding suggests that the knowledge about the possibility of conflict management alone is related

---

[6] See Leo Hamon, "Peace Research: Outline of an Inquiry into Causes, Effects, and Problems", *International Social Science Journal* (Paris), Vol. 17, No. 3, 1965, pp. 420-41.

[7] See Jules Moch, "Increasing Security Through Disarmament", in Arthur Larson, ed., *A Warless World* (New York, 1963) pp. 11-30.

to the content of peace research, that the knowledge about economic development and population control is "general social systems research", and that the knowledge about material technology is "technological and engineering research".[8] Thus peace research for him is only "transition research."[9] It is difficult to agree with this narrow interpretation of peace research. Economic development, population control, conflict management, and control of material technology are all conditions or requirements of stable peace, which, as stated earlier, is the objective of peace research. If, then, general systems research and technological and engineering research is necessary, it is so because it is an integral part of peace research itself. Knowledge, whether acquired through what Boulding calls transition research, or general systems research, or engineering research, is to be utilized for the purpose of peace. Peace research can be called transition research only if one assumes that conflict management, which, according to Boulding, is the major function of transition research, represents a temporary problem in international relationships. This assumption is not correct. The question of interrelationship between peace research and conflict will be taken up later. Suffice it to say here that the elimination of conflict is neither possible nor desirable. Therefore, even if it is granted that peace research is concerned only with conflict management, it is not possible to find out a standard solution for this problem that could be applicable at all times. New research is required as and when new types of conflict arise. Thus peace research even within its narrow framework is not a transitional but a continuous process. Actually, keeping in view the definition of peace research attempted above, we should regard peace research as a field much wider than it is supposed to be by Boulding.

II

This raises the question of the scope of peace research. A definite identification of the scope of peace research is as

[8] See Kenneth E. Boulding, "Needs and Opportunities in Peace Research and Education", *Our Generation Against Nuclear War* (Montreal), Vol. 3, No. 2, p. 25.
[9] *Ibid.*

difficult as its definition. But a few observations may be made in order to help the reader to form his own ideas about the scope of peace research. First of all, peace research touches all aspects of human life. Thus it has a close relationship with all social sciences. This relationship exists partly because of the conviction that methods of social science research are applicable in research for peace and partly because of the realization that research in social sciences is meaningless unless it is helpful in solving the problem of war and peace. Peace research is thus a movement in social sciences. It seeks to benefit from the results of social science research done so far, and it also indicates avenues for further research in social sciences. It can, no doubt, be said that all social research is relevant to some problem or the other. But the fundamental problem in peace research is peace. Therefore, the relevance of social research has to be judged in accordance with the criterion whether or not it contributes to the solution of the problem of peace. Thus all other problems with which social sciences have been dealing individually are subordinate to the basic problem of peace. By stressing this subordination of man's other problems to his problem of peace, peace research has provided a link between various social sciences, a link which has been even otherwise developing as a result of several forces unleashed by the advancement of technology. In the academic field this link has led to the adoption of what has come to be known as the interdisciplinary approach.

The essence of the interdisciplinary approach is that since a general problem is often full of complexities, no one-factor theory can explain it or prescribe solutions for it and that, therefore, it should be examined from various possible points of view. No problem can be more complex than that of peace. Therefore, all disciplines of social sciences are relevant to peace research in so far as they can be helpful in uncovering the complexities of peace. If the growth in the number of independent social sciences represents an attempt to study in detail the parts of man's problem, peace research represents a revival of the ancient belief that the parts cannot be isolated absolutely from the whole. Thus peace research is a reminder to the effect that peace, which has hitherto been neglected in the development of autonomous disciplines of social sciences, is a connecting link between those disciplines.

The scope of peace research, therefore, is very wide. It covers negatively the efforts for the understanding of conditions that may prevent violence and positively the steps necessary for the creation of conditions for the furtherance of harmonious relations among nations. The understanding of the conditions that prevent war and contribute to peace can be achieved through an interdisciplinary approach. Social science disciplines like history, political science, sociology, demography, psychology, and economics are all helpful. Thus peace research is, as Johan Galtung calls, cross-disciplinary.[10]

Special mention should be made here of the link between peace research and international relations. Although it is not yet a settled question whether international relations is a social science or not and whether it is an independent discipline or not,[11] yet peace research is inconceivable outside the context of international relations.

This is so for two reasons. One is that the concern for peace which brings various social sciences together is nowhere more relevant than in international relations and the other is that peace research represents the latest approach to the study of international relations. These two reasons have themselves assumed significance from the way in which the study of international relations has grown through various stages in the twentieth century. The first stage, which continued up to the end of the First World War, was dominated by the monopoly of diplomatic historians.[12] International relations were presented only in a descriptive and chronological manner without any reference to how various events and situations fitted into the general pattern of international behaviour. The study of

[10] Johan Galtung, "A Critical Definition of Peace Research", *Our Generation Against Nuclear War*, Vol. 3, No. 2, p. 7.

[11] The following sources are useful for this question: Waldemar Gurian, "The Study of International Relations", *Review of Politics* (Notre Dame), Vol. 8, July 1946, pp. 275-82; Institute of International Studies and Overseas Administration, *Is International Relations a Discipline?* (Eugene, Oregon, 1960); Peter A Toma, "How Autonomous is International Relations?", *International Relations* (London), Vol. 11, October 1964, pp. 670-78; and Frederick S. Dunn, "The Scope of International Relations", *World Politics* (Princeton), Vol. 1, October 1948, pp. 142-46.

[12] For details of the various stages of the growth of the study of international relations see Kenneth W. Thompson, "The Study of International Politics: A Study of Trends and Developments", *Review of Politics*, Vol. 14, October 1952, pp. 433-67.

current events was generally avoided and no attempt was made to deduce universal principles from the descriptive study of past facts. The second stage, beginning with the end of the First World War, was characterized by an emphasis on the study of current events and their interpretation from the point of view of their immediate significance. This approach was an attempt to do what had been ignored by diplomatic historians, namely the study of the present. But though it stressed the study of the present, it did not seek to establish any relationship between the post-war political problems and the comparable problems of the past. Thus the current events approach corrected the failing of diplomatic historians without retaining the useful aspect of their approach. During the interwar period, another approach was also dominant. This approach laid stress on the institutionalization of international relations through law and organization. The emphasis was inspired by the belief that international community would be able to create institutions by which all international problems would be automatically solved. Attempts were, therefore, made to search for goals and values towards which international community should progress as also to create institutions under which those goals and values could be realized. This approach was given special emphasis because of the establishment of the League of Nations. An important consequence of this approach was that it infused in scholars a zeal for visionary reformism, so much so that their concern became the creation of an ideal international society. It seemed possible that some intellectual effort coupled with missionary zeal could abolish war. This spirit did not limit itself to research but it also extended to the teaching of international relations.[13] The experience of the First World War gave impetus to the reforming spirit, and the accepted values of international life were supposed to be democracy, international understanding, arbitration, national self-determination, disarmament, and collective secu-

---

[13] It would be appropriate to quote the following from Thomas Cook and Malcolm Moos: "In the Universities, a number of student generations were taught international relations as moral principles of world peace, the potential splendors of the League, the wickedness of departure from Wilsonian doctrines, the evils of imperialism and dollar diplomacy, and the efficacy of popular demands for a better world and for a change of heart." See Thomas I. Cook and Malcolm Moos, *Power Through Purpose* (Baltimore, 1954) p. 95.

rity.[14] This stage, called the idealist stage, in the study of international relations has so often been discussed that its detailed analysis here would be superfluous.[15] Simultaneously, during the interwar period, the realist school was emerging, and it became dominant during the forties and fifties. This school insisted on international politics as a process of conflict of interest defined in terms of power.[16] In the sixties, however, the systemic school seems most likely to be prevailing. The present stage in the study of international relations has three important characteristics: a growing dissatisfaction with the state of the field, an emerging conviction that the concepts of other disciplines must be utilized, and a trend in favour of the scientific study of international relations.[17] Beyond these broad generalizations, however, there is hardly anything to unify the new trends in the study of international relations. A good deal of work is being done in the theory of international systems, moving towards what is called the international systems approach. Scholars like Morton Kaplan,[18] Thomas Schelling,[19] Anatol Rapoport,[20] Karl Deutsch,[21] Lewis Richardson,[22] Herman Kahn,[23] Quincy Wright,[24] Charles McClelland,[25]

[14] See William T.R. Fox, "Inter-War International Relations Research: The American Experience", *World Politics*, Vol. 2, October 1949, p. 70.
[15] For a detailed discussion of the idealist school, the following works would be found useful: John H. Herz, *Political Realism and Political Idealism* (Chicago, 1951); E.H. Carr, *The Twenty Years' Crisis* (London, 1961); Reinhold Niebuhr, *The Children of Light and the Children of Darkness* (New York, 1960); Kenneth W. Thompson, *Christian Ethics and the Dilemmas of Foreign Policy* (Durham, North Carolina, 1959); and Otto Klineberg, *The Human Dimensions in International Relations* (New York, 1964).
[16] For the realist school see Hans J. Morgenthau, *Politics Among Nations* (Chicago, 1959); Martin Wight, *Power Politics* (London, 1946); W.T.R. Fox, "The Reconciliation of the Desirable and the Possible", *American Scholar* (Washington D.C.), Vol. 18, Spring 1949, pp. 212-16; Quincy Wright, "Realism and Idealism in International Politics", *World Politics*, Vol. 5, October 1952, pp. 116-28; and Samuel H. Magill, "Neither Utopian Nor Realist", *Worldview* (New York), Vol. 5, September 1962, pp. 6-9.
[17] As James Rosenau observes: "Today, workers in the field...have... acquired a new language, the language of the scientific method". See James N. Rosenau, ed., *International Politics and Foreign Policy* (New York, 1961) p. 7.
[18] Morton Kaplan, *System and Process in International Politics* (New York, 1957).
[19] Thomas C. Schelling, *The Strategy of Conflict* (Cambridge, Mass., 1960).
[20] Anatol Rapoport, *Fights, Games, and Debates* (Ann Arbor, 1960).
[21] Karl W. Deutsch, *Nationalism and Social Communication* (Cambridge, Mass., 1953).
[22] Lewis F. Richardson, *Arms and Insecurity* (Pittsburgh, 1960).
[23] Herman Kahn, *Thinking About the Unthinkable* (New York, 1962).
[24] Quincy Wright, *A Study of War* (Chicago, 1965).
[25] Charles A. McClelland, *Theory and the International System* (New York, 1966).

and Kenneth Boulding[26] have done commendable work with the international systems approach. Their writings represent a new movement in the field of international studies with the objective of making the study of international systems more and more interdisciplinary and theoretical. This movement seeks to improve international studies so far made merely with the approaches of diplomatic history and current events. Research is thus in progress in a number of countries in order to discover a theoretical order in international systems.

But the interest of most of the scholars engaged in this kind of research is essentially purely academic. The concern for peace is not as such uppermost in their minds. This concern, of course, is reflected in another research movement in the field of international studies, a research movement which Kenneth Boulding calls the conflict studies movement.[27] Those working in this movement are guided by the perception that conflict is a phenomenon characteristic of all social systems and that conflict processes, in so far as they exhibit common patterns, can be fruitfully studied for developing a general theory of conflict. Such an exercise in theory-building is based upon the hope that the insights drawn from the study of one form of conflict can be applied to the resolution of another form of conflict. The Centre for Research on Conflict Resolution, University of Michigan, and the Polemologische Institute, Groningen (the Netherlands), are among the chief centres of research representing the conflict studies movement.[28] The third dimension to current research in international relations is provided by the concern for national security. This kind of research views national security as the most important problem in international system. It is an attempt at deploying intellectual resources in the interest of a particular nation's defence, and its main areas of investigation, therefore, are armaments, military balance, strategy, and defence policy. The Rand Corporation, the Hudson Institute, and the Institute for Strategic Studies may be mentioned as among the principal

[26] Kenneth E. Boulding, *Conflict and Defense* (New York, 1963).
[27] See Kenneth E. Boulding, "Reality Testing and Value Orientation in International Systems: The Role of Research", *International Social Science Journal*, Vol. 17, No. 3, 1965, p. 413.
[28] For a list of various other institutions engaged in conflict studies and for the nature of their work see Appendices.

organizations engaged in national security research.[29]

What distinguishes these three trends in the study of international relations one from another is their motivation. The general systems approach is inspired by the desire to seek a theoretical order in international relations, the conflict studies approach is guided by the need for a general theory of conflict, and the national security approach is motivated by strategic considerations of security. Indirectly all these three approaches may be viewed as approaches to peace. But concern for peace is not direct except in the case of the conflict studies approach. The general systems approach is purely academic, whereas the national security approach takes too narrow a concept of security. The difference in these approaches to the study of international relations is mainly due to the partial character of the understanding of the problem of peace. The historians before the First World War thought that peace could be preserved if the follies of the past were avoided. They based their study of international relations, which they identified with diplomatic history, on the notion that history repeats itself. Under the influence of the current events approach, peace was viewed as a matter of the control of the present. The idealists put too high a premium on moral forces and the institutions of law and organization. An understanding of history, the control of the present, and the strengthening of law and organization have thus been the suggestions resulting from academic inquiry into the causes of war and conditions of peace.

Peace research as an approach to international relations is different from other approaches not because these suggestions are wrong but because they are mutually exclusive. The first thing that peace research seeks to do, therefore, is to establish an interrelationship between various approaches to the study of international relations that developed before the Second World War on the one hand and in recent years on the other. The approach of peace research insists that the other approaches take an incomplete view of international relations. For they do not take into account the goal towards which international society has progressed or should progress. It is this basic question which imparts a new dimension to the study of inter-

---

[29] For other institutions of this type see Appendices.

national relations. By virtue of its emphasis on peace, peace research is concerned with the evolution of peaceful international relations which is the fulfilment of the nature of international society. As such, a distinguishing mark of the study of international relations by the peace research approach would be a stress on the nature of international society.

Peace research takes a deterministic view of the nature of international society inasmuch as international society is seen as gradually progressing towards the attainment of peace. This is essentially a matter of the evolution of world community. A partial definition of peace research can, therefore, be that it is the sum total of intellectual resources and their application in facilitating the process of the evolution of world community. Thus peace research seeks to impart a purpose to the study of international relations, namely the avoidance of war and the maintenance of peace. That is why John Burton goes further and says that the recent breakthrough in the field of international relations and the growing concern for peace will soon make the distinction between international relations and peace research disappear.[30] But so long as the distinction exists, peace research can be described as the *purposive study of international relations*. The purpose is obviously peace which peace research seeks to raise to the status of a value. If, then, international relations and peace research can be called a science, the former is a value-free science and the latter a value science.

III

This raises two important questions. One, whether peace research is or has the promise of becoming a science and, two, whether peace research can be identified with peace movements in view of the fact that the latter also take peace as a value.

The claim of peace research to being a science can be examined by referring to the distinction that exists in the twentieth-century use of the terms "philosophy", "science", and "theory". The words "twentieth-century use" must be noted. For it is only after the advent of the twentieth

---

[30] John W. Burton, "Peace Research and International Relations", *Journal of Conflict Resolution* (Chicago), Vol. 8, September 1964, pp. 281-86.

century that the controversy has arisen about the meaning of the three terms. Up to the end of the nineteenth century all major contributions made to knowledge were concerned with general questions about the nature of man, his goal of life, and the means to realize the goal. In asking questions of this type, pronouncements were freely made on good and evil, morally right and wrong, just and unjust. In support of their conclusions, the writers would draw upon the sources of religion or natural law. The answers that were given to questions pertaining to man and his affairs were considered scientific. With the beginning of the twentieth century, however, scholars became aware of limitations in the nature of science, and they found that the essential tools of science were observation of facts, measurement, and logical reasoning. Any conclusion that could not be supported on the basis of these tools could not, therefore, be called scientific. The new insistence on scientific methods gave rise to the theoretical opinion that no scientific choice between ultimate values can be made. The scientist was declared unable to determine the superiority of any ends or purposes over any other ends or purposes in absolute terms. Statements concerning values, therefore, were viewed merely as personal opinions, and support for value systems as such was considered beyond the reach of science. For no value system can be justified purely on grounds of observation, measurement, and logical reasoning. The result was that even the democratic system of values, scientifically speaking, was considered merely as a dogma, or ideology, or what Robert MacIver would call "myth"[31]. Albert Einstein even went to the extent of declaring that even the extirpation of the human race cannot be refuted scientifically if somebody approves of it as a goal.[32]

This decisive change in the meaning of science has left its impact on the meaning of philosophy and theory also. The growing demand for precision has made it necessary to distinguish between science and philosophy; the original meaning of the latter had been all-inclusive and coextensive with that

---

[31] Robert M. MacIver, *The Web of Government* (New York, 1947) pp. 39 and 51.
[32] Albert Einstein, "Freedom and Science", in Ruth N. Anshen, ed., *Freedom: Its Meaning* (New York, 1940) p. 382.

of science. From its classical beginnings, the term "philosophy" implied a universalistic reference. It dealt with general ideas about the world, man, and God. Thus it was in the realm of philosophy to explain everything. It was not limited to the physical world, but it extended even to metaphysical questions and was also supposed to engage in speculation which is now considered beyond the reach of the tools of science.

Theory, it is generally agreed, is a proposition or a set of propositions that explains something[33]. Philosophy explains everything, but theory explains only something. Whether a theory is scientific or not depends on whether the tools of science have been used in explaining the phenomenon with which a particular theory may be concerned. Thus philosophy can be called theory in so far as it explains a phenomenon, and it can be called science in so far as it applies scientific methods. This interrelationship between science, theory, and philosophy is of utmost significance for an examination of the question whether peace research is a science or not.

Opinion, however, is divided on this question. There are those who have made out a strong case for peace research as a science,[34] and there are those who believe that peace research is not, and can never become, a science.[35] Still others hold that peace research should be treated as a part of the science of international relations[36]. Some of the supporters of the view that peace research is a science have chosen to call it "science of peace". But the question of peace research as a science has not been examined in the new perspective created by the change in the meaning of science and the resultant inter-

[33] There are, however, various views on the meaning of theory. For details of those views see William J. Goode and Paul K. Klatt, *Methods in Social Research* (New York, 1952); David Easton, *The Political System: An Inquiry into the State of Political Science* (New York, 1953); Thomas P. Jenkin, *The Study of Political Theory* (Garden City, N.Y., 1955); George H. Sabine, "What Is a Political Theory?", *Journal of Politics* (Gainesville), Vol. 1, 1939, pp. 1-16; and William A. Glaser, "The Types and Uses of Political Theory", *Social Research* (New York), Vol. 22, Autumn, 1955, pp. 275-96.

[34] See, for example, Theo. F. Lentz, *Towards a Science of Peace* (New York, 1955); W. Fred Cottrell, "Men Cry Peace", in Institute for Social Research (Oslo), *Research for Peace Essays* (Amsterdam, 1954) pp. 99-162.

[35] See Leo Hamon, "Peace Research: Outline of an Inquiry into Causes, Effects, and Problems", *International Social Science Journal*, Vol. 17, No. 3, 1965, pp. 420-41.

[36] This was the view taken by some of the participants in the prize contest organized by the Institute for Social Research, Oslo, on the relevance of scientific research in the peaceful solution of international conflicts.

relationship between science, theory, and philosophy, referred to above.

It is the submission of this writer that peace research can develop into a science. There can be possibly two objections to this statement. One, that since peace research takes peace as an ultimate value and since no value can be provided by scientific methods, peace research cannot be a science; and, two, that peace with which peace research is so intimately connected is not a problem for science. The first objection is based upon the assumption that values can have no scientific basis, and the other objection flows from the belief that peace is not a question of providing more scientific knowledge but one of applying whatever knowledge we already have. The assumption on which the first objection is based is inapplicable to peace research, and the belief from which the second objection flows is wrong. An attempt to show how that assumption is inapplicable and how that belief is wrong will not only negatively meet the objections to peace research as a science but will also positively explain how peace research is or can become a science.

The basic point made by the supporters[37] of the scientific method is that science cannot prove the validity of any purpose or value, nor can it state in absolute terms which of several conflicting purposes or values is better than others except in relation to some presupposed goal or idea which may have been either grasped by faith and intuition or built up on religious foundations. The scientific method cannot provide conclusive scientific evidence in favour of such a presupposed goal or idea. It only enables us to find out which particular value may be preferable in relative terms. As such, anyone committed to the scientific method can libel the foundations of peace research as a set of prejudices or a set of unverifiable hypotheses. For peace is a matter of value and the man of scientific knowledge, as Vernon Van Dyke asserts,[38] is bound

---

[37] See, for example, Barbara Wooton, *Testament for Social Science: An Essay in the Application of Scientific Method* (New York, 1951); F.S.C. Northrop, *The Logic of Science and the Humanities* (New York, 1947); Felix Kaufmann, *Methodology of the Social Sciences* (New York, 1944); and John Madge, *The Tools of Social Science* (London, 1953).

[38] Vernon Van Dyke, *Political Science: A Philosophical Analysis* (London, 1960).

to be neutral because he cannot prove any value on the basis of intersubjective transmissibility. Let it be remembered, however, that the scientific method does not deny that there is no such thing as an absolute value. It only underlines that it cannot be proved or disproved intersubjectively. If, therefore, peace as a value is not scientifically supportable, it is not scientifically unsupportable either. But peace as a value is not only not scientifically unsupportable but is also scientifically supportable to an extent. Science differs from philosophy essentially in terms of a wide gap between their scope, inasmuch as science deals with a particular part of reality as it exists in the present, and philosophy is concerned with total reality as it existed in the past, as it exists in the present, and as it may exists in the future. As such, the question of values is relevant to science only in the present. If, then, science applies the test of intersubjective transmissibility to the value of peace, it can do so only with a view to finding out whether peace as a value is scientifically supportable in the present. In order to prove the scientific validity of peace as a value, the test of intersubjective transmissibility can be met by the fact that there is now a general agreement available on the value of peace which never existed before. Science after all is concerned with that on which universal agreement can be obtained.[39] Universal agreement, of course, is not acceptable to some writers[40] as a scientific proof. Arnold Brecht, for example, holds that reference to agreement, besides being an unscientific proof, does not help where there is no agreement[41]. This contention may be relevant in the case of other values but not in that of peace. For peace today is not a value on which there may be dissenters. The values which scholars tried to uphold in the past were justice, security, order, freedom, equality, and the general welfare as the end of state and government. Peace was never taken to be a field for any

---

[39] Norman Campbell, *What is Science?* (New York, 1952) p. 27.
[40] John Dewey says: "A proposition does not gain validity because of the number of persons who accept it". Vide John Dewey, *Logic: The Theory of Inquiry* (New York, 1949) p. 490, note 4. Similarly Hayek observes: "The general intellectual atmosphere of the time is always determined by the views on which the opposing scholars agree". Vide F.A. Hayek, *The Counter-Revolution of Science* (Glencoe, 1954) p. 191.
[41] Arnold Brecht, *Political Theory: The Foundations of Twentieth-Century Political Thought* (Princeton, 1959) p. 11.

rigorous intellectual exercise. At best it found place in the pronouncements of sages and seers. As stated earlier, peace did not attain the status of ultimate value in the study of international relations until after the Second World War. The reason has been the lack of universal agreement about peace as a value. Whatever schemes and efforts are currently under way for building a peaceful world order are based upon a faith in the value of peace. And scientists seeking to discover prospects for peace could do so only in terms of evidence of growing and effective acceptance of peace as a value. The evidence about universal agreement is empirical. For such an agreement can be obtainable only on those propositions which are susceptible of tests of logic and observation. Science asserts that nothing that is outside observation can be called science.[42] But the fact about universal agreement on peace as a value is observable. Moreover, as James Conant rightly holds, the essence of science lies in the contribution that each scientific development makes to further development.[43] If, therefore, science has been unable to justify any value in the past, it does not mean that it cannot justify any value in the present or future. Science is an enterprise involving continuous probing into the unknown.[44] The theoretical opinion that no scientific choice between ultimate values can be made arose mainly because of the lack of universal agreement about this choice at the beginning of the twentieth century. The result was the inability of science to condemn morally Bolshevism, Fascism, or National Socialism. This inability has been gradually declining after the Second World War partly as a result of emerging general agreement on peace as a value and partly because of the change in the criterion of moral condemnation. The moral condemnation of any totalitarian system, which the scientific method could not provide, had to be the basis of difference in ideologies on which no universal

[42] Jacob Bronowski, *The Common Sense of Science* (Cambridge, 1953) p. 70.
[43] James B. Conant, *Science and Common Sense* (Englewood Cliffs, 1957) pp. 219-20.
[44] *Ibid.* Collingwood takes a similar view: "It (science) consists in fastening upon something we do not know, and trying to discover it.... Science is finding things out". Vide R.G. Collingwood, *The Idea of History* (Oxford, 1946) p. 9. See also Charles S. Hyneman, *The Study of Politics* (Urbana, 1959), Chapters V and IX.

agreement was possible. But now, moral condemnation of anything has to be based on the consideration whether it goes against the value of peace on which universal agreement is available. The essence of science is observation and testability. But the results of observation and test are not static. Observation and test are only tools of science, and the results yielded by them may change. "Each generation", observes A.N. Whitehead, "criticizes the unconscious assumptions made by its parents."[45] From this emerges new truth. What science may have found out in the past may not be borne out by facts in the present. To say that peace as a value has no scientific validity would, therefore, be an unscientific statement. For it would imply that the results obtained in the past are valid for all time; and that is what runs counter to the basis of science which insists on continuous search after reality through scientific tools.

Thus peace research presents a reminder of the real meaning of science and discovers for itself a scientific validity for its basic value. But peace research is concerned not merely with a theoretical espousal of peace but also with its practical realization. The relationship between science and practice is a less controversial question. For the main function of science is to contribute to knowledge which may be utilized in the realization of an ideal. The relevant question here is whether science can improve our knowledge about the causes of war and conditions of peace. The present writer submits that a body of verified knowledge applicable to the problems of peaceful adjustments in international relations does not exist and that such a knowledge can be acquired scientifically.

There are three requirements which a body of knowledge has to fulfil for being called scientific: verifiability, systematization, and generality. A proposition is said to be verified when it has been checked and approved of by many specialists in the relevant field. But scientific knowledge is sometimes considered as certain or exact rather than verifiable; and since certainty or exactness is a logical impossibility, scientists deal with probabilities rather than with certainties.[46] In order to

[45] A.N. Whitehead, *Science and the Modern World* (New York, 1925) p. 36.
[46] Hans Reichenbach, *The Rise of Scientific Philosophy* (Berkeley, 1951) pp. 27-49, 229-49.

fulfil the requirement of verifiability, science must be empirical and it must be reliable.[47] The second requirement, that of systematization, is met when knowledge is organized into an intelligible pattern with significant relationships made clear. Concern for system implies that scientists want to proceed from particular towards general facts or, in other words, from knowledge of isolated facts towards knowledge of connections between facts. Thus the ideal of science, as Morris Cohen and Ernest Nagel believe, is to achieve a systematic interconnection of facts[48]. The third requirement is that a verifiable and systematic knowledge of interconnection between facts should be able to make generalizations so as to facilitate explanation and prediction, which are among the chief functions of science.

Let us now see how far these requirements are met by peace research. As for verifiability, it can be safely maintained that the needed knowledge about the causes of war and conditions of peace is verifiable. For the basic objective of peace research is to use the scientifically acquired knowledge for the avoidance of the causes of war and the recreation of conditions that contribute to peace. Neither this avoidance nor this recreation is possible unless propositions built on the basis of empirical study of past and present hold true in future also. In other words, specialists in the field must accept the view that the methods can be depended upon to produce trustworthy results. There are a number of fields which can be probed by the scientific method and the knowledge thus gained may be fruitfully used in the service of peace. Even international relations provide good material for such a probe. We know, for example, that despite a good many serious conflicts there has been no major war after 1945. What is it that has prevented conflicts from degenerating into a general war? This question can be examined from the point of view of both cause and effect. To identify what could be other such questions for

---

[47] Carl J. Friedrich, "Political Philosophy and the Science of Politics", in Roland Young, ed., *Approaches to the Study of Politics* (Evanston, 1958) pp. 174-75. See also Alfred Jules Ayer, *Language: Truth and Logic* (New York, n.d.) p. 100.

[48] Morris R. Cohen and Ernest Nagel, *An Introduction to Logic and Scientific Method* (New York, 1934) p. 394.

investigation[49] is itself an important task of peace research. Thus the identification of relevant problems and their examination are both susceptible of scientific inquiry. Questions of war and peace can be made answerable through the process of observation because war and peace are matters of human behaviour.

The results yielded by scientific inquiry have obviously to be put in a meaningful framework if they are to be utilized in the interest of peace. In other words, the knowledge about war and peace has to be systematized by seeking out similarities and differences and by putting the like things together. While looking for similarities and differences, peace research has also to look for relationships, whether correlations or causal relations. It must establish what is related to what, both within and among the categories of its classification scheme. This kind of systematization is the work of intelligence, and the free and utmost use of intelligence, as P.W. Bridgman believes, is science.[50] From this point of view, the science of peace could perhaps be defined as a body of knowledge resulting from the application of disciplined curiosity and collective intellectual effort to formulate, develop, and progressively answer questions relevant to peace with the help of purposeful observation and reason. When peace researchers have developed such a body of knowledge, peace research will have attained the status of science.

The difficulty, however, arises in regard to the requirement of generality which, as already pointed out, demands that we should go to higher and higher levels of generalization and should be able to employ concepts and make statements that apply to more and more objects, instances, and events. On the ability to perform this task depends the capacity of explanation and prediction. But predictive propositions may be unverifiable because of the selective nature of supporting

---

[49] A commendable effort in this direction has been made by Theo F. Lentz in a chapter "Outlining the Research" contributed to his *Towards a Science of Peace*, pp. 119-49; by Leo Hamon in his article "Peace Research: Outline of an Inquiry, Causes, Effects, and Problems", *International Social Science Journal*, Vol. 17, No. 3, pp. 420-41; by W. Fred Cottrell in his "Men Cry Peace" contributed to *Research For Peace Essays*, pp. 99-162; and by Ch. Boasson in his paper "The Relevance of Research to the Problems of Peace" contributed to *Ibid.*, pp. 165-251.

[50] Quoted by Theo F. Lentz in his *Towards a Science of Peace*, p. 106.

evidence and the variety of human desires and rules of action. A venture to make predictions at a high level of generality may, therefore, be hazardous.[51] Thus the greatest obstacle to a scientific study of not only peace but of any social phenomenon stems from possible incompatibility between the requirement of verifiability and the requirement of generality. Hence scientists have to confine themselves to those propositions that are verifiable at low levels of generality. This limitation of scientists is nowhere more relevant than in the field of peace research. But it is in this very field that a start can be made to curb this limitation. At present the concern of peace research is to investigate into causes of war and conflict in all possible areas of human relations. It should take up at this stage only those questions that can be handled quantitatively, and care about generality should be taken only in so far as it is permissible by the requirement of verifiability. It should aim at a structure of knowledge that is trustworthy but limited rather than at a structure that is comprehensive but untrustworthy. The behavioural approach comes closest to the acceptance of the limitation of science, and hence it emphasizes the importance of the scientific method mainly in terms of verifiability. This emphasis has led to the emergence of quantitative methods. But whereas behaviourism is too much occupied with verifiability and quantitative methods, peace research cannot put so much premium on verifiability as to ignore generality altogether. The present stage of peace research can no doubt be concerned with the use of the instrument of verifiability in order to discover all possible dimensions of war and conflict and peace. But the ideal should be the development of such a science of peace that all laws, propositions, and facts can be deduced from it[52] and which can contribute to the concept of the unity of science propounded by A. Wolf.[53]

The concept of the unity of science is very significant to peace research. It is in this context that the element of value again becomes relevant. Peace as a value points out the purpose for which scientific studies should be made. If peace

[51] See Social Science Research Council, Committee on Historiography, *Theory and Practice in Historical Study* (New York, 1946) pp. 138-39.
[52] Philipp Frank, *Philosophy of Science* (Englewood Cliffs, 1957) p. 42.
[53] See the definition by A. Wolf quoted by Wilson Gee in his *Social Science Research Methods* (New York, 1950) pp. 156-57.

is the basic problem, then even the traditional social sciences will have to be studied in reference to that problem. It should, therefore, be an imperative for the growth of peace research as a science to establish a link between various partial theories of peace and conflict so that a general theory may emerge. The establishment of this link and the emergence of a general theory can both be possible when the interrelationship between science, theory, and philosophy, referred to above, is recognized. Theory in its partial character would discover laws of explanation about conflict and peace in various situations, and philosophy would relate those various theories to the supreme objective of man, namely peace. The result would be a general theory which in its purest form is nothing else but a science. But since peace itself is meaningless except in the context of the totality of man, peace research would not only be scientific in the sense that universal agreement is available on peace as a value but also philosophic in the sense that it covers the whole realm of man's life. Peace research thus admits of no conflict between science and philosophy. It rather proceeds further from even W.E. Hocking's suggestion that science and philosophy should be given those aspects that are amenable in their own respective fields.[54] Peace research does not approve of any isolation between the realm of science and the realm of philosophy. It neither aims at making science more philosophic as Jacques Maritain and Eric Voegelin tried to, nor seeks to make philosophy more scientific as scholars like Edmund Husserl have done.[55] It should only aim at making a proper use of both science and philosophy in order to acquire relevant knowledge to be utilized in the service of peace. It can thus be called a philosophical science as well as a scientific philosophy. It is here that the distinction between *nomothetic science* and *ideographic science* drawn by David Smith[56] may be of some use. The former refers to the search for the abstract, whereas the latter deals with temporal events. Peace research combines both these aspects. It deals

---

[54] See W.E. Hocking, *Science and the Idea of God* (Chapel Hill, 1944) p. 4.

[55] See Jacques Maritain, *Man and the State* (Chicago, 1951); Eric Voegelin, *The New Science of Politics* (Chicago, (1952); and Alfred Schutz, *Philosophy and Phenomenological Research* (1953).

[56] See David G. Smith, "Political Science and Political Theory", *American Political Science Review*, Vol. 51, September 1957, p. 735.

with the abstract which falls within the realm of philosophy, and it also deals with the temporal which falls within the realm of science.

The development of the science of peace research along the lines suggested above is not, however, possible in a short time. It will be possible only when an integration of various theories is made. The development of a science proceeds along two stages: clear identification of a problem and the growth of reliable knowledge for the solution of that problem. By identifying peace as a problem, peace research has completed the first stage. It has also entered the second stage, but it has yet to complete that stage.

With the completion of the second stage peace research will have attained the status of a complete science and, consequently, that of an independent discipline also. In fact, peace research is likely to go even further than achieving the status of an independent subject of study. By insisting on peace as the supreme value, peace research offers a possibility of developing itself into a master discipline or an umbrella science. In that case, traditional social sciences, which already enjoy the status of independent disciplines, would be reduced to the status of subordinate sciences or sub-disciplines. The trend may even grow still further and cover natural sciences too. Quite many scholars drawn from disciplines of the pure sciences have done commendable work in the field of peace research. Their growing interest in and concern for peace are an indication that research in the pure sciences also may acquire purposiveness in relation to peace.[57] It should not be surprising, then, if the development of peace research as a complete science leads to a diminution of academic independence of the pure sciences also.

In any case, the development of the science of peace has to proceed in all possible directions. Its purpose can be served only when it is used at all levels, the most important of which is the formulation of national policies. The reason why this level is most important is the obvious fact that international

---

[57] The responsibility of scholars of the pure sciences for the cause of peace has been pointed out by a number of eminent writers. See, for example, Aldous Huxley, *Science, Liberty, and Peace* (London, 1947) pp. 49-63; Thorstein Veblen, *Place of Science in Modern Civilization* (New York, 1961).

wars are in most cases the result of national policies. Traditionally national governments have viewed war as the rational extension of diplomacy. But peace research would view war as an irrational social phenomenon which can be controlled with scientific knowledge. To seek a change in national policies, therefore, it is necessary that a change is brought about in the concept of war at the governmental, official level. The relationship between peace research and government policy is obviously bound to be of a tenuous nature. But peace research can gradually exert its influence on policy formulation, and this can be done in two ways. One is to suggest such alternatives to war as can perform the same functions as hitherto performed by war, and the other is to help reducing the compulsions that lead policy-makers to choose warlike policies. The extent to which peace research can influence national policies would, therefore, depend upon its ability to suggest such alternatives and reduce such compulsions. Reduction of compulsions, however, is something with which peace research is concerned indirectly. For compulsions on policy-makers are mainly from public opinion, in the formation of which peace resrarch cannot have a direct role. As a science, peace research would only produce knowledge which can be utilized in both policy formulation and opinion formation. But in policy formulation the role of peace research is more direct because a large number of foreign policy departments in the world now have research units in which the research programme might be geared to the requirements of peace. Peace research cannot directly participate in the formation of public opinion. It can only stress that the formation of public opinion in favour of peace is necessary and can suggest what kind of public opinion would contribute to peace. The actual task of opinion formation will have to be performed by persons other than those engaged in peace research.

IV

This brings us to the question of distinction between peace research and the peace movement. Though peace research and the peace movement are both concerned with peace, the two differ in their approach and mode of operation. The peace movement represents a demand for peace arising from ethical conviction that war is a moral evil and from the pragmatic consideration that war in modern times is not going to pay. Often, behind the peace movement are heterogeneous groups consisting of people who believe in different kinds of measures to obtain peace. Historically, this movement has taken place in almost all parts of the world. It can be divided into two categories: the first category relates to the resistance offered to unjust governmental regimes in order to seek redress of certain grievances by peaceful means, and the second to the evolution of peaceful international order for the realization of the ideal of peace as such. The former can be called passive resistance, and the latter can be called the peace movement, though rather only loosely.[58] In the strict sense anything which works for the ideal of abolishing war and achieving peace without necessarily involving specific issues is a part of the peace movement. Immanuel Kant's scheme for perpetual peace and the work done by several organizations during the First World War[59] for the establishment of a general international organization can thus be regarded as a part of the peace movement. After the Second World War, the peace movement has gained added significance. It is going on strongly in several countries, notably Norway, Canada, Japan, Britain, and France. Several groups[60] are functioning in these countries to help in the creation of opinion against war.

What distinguishes these peace movements from passive resistance movements is the difference in the nature of their scope inasmuch as the former is related to the general problem of war and peace and the latter to specific manifestations of that problem. As such, the Negroes' struggle for civil rights

[58] A few good studies are available on resistance movements involving use of nonviolent action: Fenner A. Brockway, *Non-Cooperation in Other Lands* (Madras, 1921); Anna Ruth Fry, *Victories Without Violence* (London, 1957); C.M. Case, *Non-violent Coercion* (London, 1923); Bart De Light, *The Conquest of Violence* (London, 1937); William Robert Miller, *Nonviolence: A Christian Interpretation* (London, 1965); Frank Russell, *Theories of International Relations*; and Gene Sharp, "81 Cases of Non-violent Action", in *Civilian Defence* (London, 1964).
[59] For details of the work of such organizations see Ruhl J. Bartlett, *The League to Enforce Peace* (Chapel Hill, 1944); Gerard J. Mangone, *A Short History of International Organization* (New York, 1954); S.J. Hemleben, *Plans for World Peace Through Six Centuries* (Chicago, 1943); and C.K. Webster, *The Congress of Vienna* (New York, 1919).
[60] For details about such groups see Appendices.

currently going on in the United States is a passive resistance movement rather than a peace movement.

Thus we have three types of movements relevant to peace today: the passive resistance movement, the peace movement, and the peace research movement. Passive resistance is essentially a peaceful technique for the prevention of injustice in concrete situations. Its faith in peace is reflected mainly in the desire to avoid the use of violence, and its contribution to peace theoretically can be upheld only on the premise that the prevention of each particular injustice for which passive resistance is used is a step towards peace. On the other hand, the peace movement, which is concerned with the general problem of war, survives on one-factor theories. Its time perspective is short, and it has a tendency to proceed on what Johan Galtung[61] calls an apocalyptic theory of social change in the sense that change should be brought about suddenly and completely. It sees international relations in terms of complete change. Thus the peace movement has often crystallized around specific mono-ideas like "world law", "world government", and "world decentralization". The idea of total unilateralism has also been supported vigorously by those participating in the peace movement. The inspiration for this idea has come from the writings of persons like Victor Gollancz[62] and Lewis Mumford[63] and some Quakers[64] who have argued in favour of unilateralism from a moral, religious, and pacifist point of view. It has also been supported by men like Bertrand Russell,[65] Stephen King-Hall,[66] and C. Wright Mills.[67] The second group is not opposed to the use of force as such, but is uncompromisingly against the thermonuclear war and any preparation for it. The approach adopted by the first group towards unilateralism is moral, and the approach adopted by the second group is essentially pragmatic, even though a certain

---

[61] Johan Galtung, "A Critical Definition of Peace Research", p. 15.
[62] See Victor Gollancz, *Devil's Reportoire or Nuclear Bombing and the Life of Man* (London, 1958).
[63] See Lewis Mumford, *The Human Way Out* (Pendle Hill Pamphlet No. 97, Wallingford, Pa., 1958).
[64] American Friends Service Committee, *Speak Truth to Power: Quaker Search for an Alternative to Balance* (1955).
[65] See Bertrand Russell, *Common Sense and Nuclear Warfare* (London, 1959).
[66] See Stephen King-Hall, *Defence in the Nuclear Age* (London, 1958).
[67] See C. Wright Mills, *The Causes of World War Three* (New York, 1959).

element of moralism is inseparable from the pragmatic approach too. In order to achieve its objective the peace movement can move in any possible direction and can suggest or take any initiative. It has, for example, often called top meetings and conferences and has suggested new proposals for resolving current conflicts. It must, however, be stated in fairness to the peace movement that organizations like the Red Cross, the League of Nations, the United Nations, and the International Court of Justice were conceived and borne by peace movements.

Thus the perspective and field of operation of the peace movement are wider than those of the passive resistance movement. Instead of taking up a particular crisis situation, the peace movement seeks to make inroads on public opinion and official policy. The resolution of a crisis or the settlement of a dispute is important for the peace movement because it might be necessary for the preservation of peace. Yet both the passive resistance movement and the peace movement survive in the realm of practical action. This ability to survive in the realm of practical action is what provides the main distinguishing mark between passive resistance and the peace movement on the one hand and peace research on the other. It is true that much of the motivation behind the peace movement is shared by peace research and vice versa. But, as the earlier treatment should show, peace research is a movement in social sciences. As such, its concern is not action alone. It is certainly not the primary concern at least. As a science its chief function is to produce knowledge of the causes of war and conflict as also of conditions of peace. Since no scientific knowledge can depend upon single-factor theories, peace research is against any deterministic view about the causes of war. Instead, its emphasis is on discovering all possible causes of war and dealing with them all. Whereas peace movement seeks to achieve peace by means of propaganda, peace research seeks to achieve it by making scientific knowledge available. Peace movement is based upon the assumption that peace is a matter of creating an awareness of the significance of peace at both popular and official levels, whereas peace research takes the existence of this awareness for granted and proceeds further in order to fulfil the intellectual responsibility created by that awareness. In so far as this awareness is the result of peace movement, the contribution of the peace movement towards providing ground for peace research must be acknowledged. The first step that peace research takes in the fulfilment of intellectual responsibility is to have faith in the assumption that war and peace are complex phenomena, that they are attributable not to one but to various factors, and that our efforts to deal with them should go in various directions simultaneously. Contrary to the peace movement, therefore, peace research adopts a multi-dimensional approach.

It is, however, not in the peace movement alone that the tendency to depend on one-factor theories is visible. To an extent it is manifest in the academic field also. Concepts like "world government" and "disarmament", around which a good deal of research has been, and is being, done, are indicative of this tendency in scholarly writings. It would, therefore, not to be correct to say that whatever research is currently under way in the name of peace can be called peace research discharging the intellectual responsibility created by the awareness of the problem of peace. For reliance on any single cause of war and on any single condition of peace even in research runs counter to the basis of scientific inquiry. Peace research, therefore, is different not only from non-academic efforts like the peace movement, but also from those academic efforts that thrive on single-factor theories.

But this is not to say that the peace movement is absolutely useless or that it does not have anything to give to, or take from, peace research. Both passive resistance and the peace movement provide the field from which peace research can pick up clues for building hypotheses and tentative propositions. It can also receive from the peace movement detailed information about the practical problems which the men engaged in the peace movement are likely to perceive better. Similar assistance may be obtained from passive resistance movements also. On the other hand, peace research can also give to the peace movement a sense of responsibility to develop the implications of its own ideas. The peace movement can utilize the theoretically derived knowledge provided by peace research. If this interconnection between passive resistance, the peace movement, and peace research is kept in mind, then it would be difficult to agree with Kenneth Boulding when he says that peace research must remain independent of the peace movement.[68] Boulding argues that peace research must follow the dynamics of science rather than that of political action.[69] His argument is valid. For peace research as a science can develop only by proceeding along the lines of scientific inquiry. But in order to develop as a science, peace research does not have to remain absolutely independent of either passive resistance or the peace movement. Earlier we tried to explain the significance of the amalgamation of applied research and pure research for peace. This amalgamation is not possible if peace research is kept in isolation from the peace movement. The two can no doubt have different fields of operation. But they are complementary to each other in so far as the ultimate objective of achieving peace is concerned. The peace movement and passive resistance can represent the applied part. And peace research can infuse some sense of sobriety into the peace movement which often adopts a sentimental approach. This is not to say that the peace movement should not care for propaganda against war and in favour of peace or that it should abandon its function of creating an awareness of the problem of peace. What is intended is that the creation of this awareness is incomplete if it only emphasizes that the problem of peace exists without suggesting how to solve it. In order to present before people the possible solutions, the peace movement has to learn a good deal from peace research. For the ability to present solutions depends upon an understanding of the causes of war which it is the purpose of peace research to produce. If the knowledge produced by peace research is used by the peace movement, it will not only make the popular awareness about the problem of peace more scientific and less sentimental but also provide opportunity for the emergence of new ideas in the form of popular reactions that can be taken up by peace research as hypotheses for further investigation. In that case, peace research will have as much to gain from the peace movement as the latter might have to gain from the former. On the other hand, the peaceful techniques

---

[68] See Kenneth E. Boulding, "The Possibilities of Peace Research in Australia", *Australian Outlook* (Melbourne), Vol. 18, August 1964, pp. 165-69.
[69] *Ibid.*, p. 156.

of resolving conflicts suggested by peace research might be applied in crisis situations by passive resistance movements. Thus passive resistance and peace movement are both necessary for the development of a complete science of peace research itself because it is through them that the requirements of testability and generality may be fulfilled. Passive resistance provides scope for testing theoretical propositions advanced by peace research, whereas the peace movement can create conditions for the consolidation of general agreement about peace as a value.

In the foregoing pages an attempt has been made to examine the present state of peace research. The emphasis on "the present state" has been laid because of the fact that peace research is not yet in any settled state. It is struggling to give a shape to itself. Therefore, whatever possible dimensions of a definition of peace research have been referred to in this chapter are those that flow as indications from the efforts of men currently engaged in peace research. The present writer has, however, tried to define peace research not only in the context of what it actually is at present but also in that of what it should become in the future.

CHAPTER TWO

Possibilities of Peace Research In India

It was stated in the first chapter that peace research has the potentiality of developing into a science and that if it so develops, it will be a value science, in the sense that the knowledge released by it will not only be utilized for peace but will also be sought with a view to utilizing it for that purpose. This double-edged purposiveness is the basis on which peace research can emerge as a complete science. As the development of a complete science will be in direct proportion to the achievement of increasingly greater generality about the laws of war and peace, peace research has no national or regional frontiers to its field of inquiry. It may be conducted in any area and in any walk of life. Therefore, when we talk of possibilities of peace research in India, it is clear that the attempt to harness those possibilities (whatever they might be) is likely to contribute to the growth of peace research as a science. National peace research, as it might be called, is not possible in complete isolation from what might be called international peace research. Julius Stone has spoken of "the nationalization of truth". Peace research in each country can help in counteracting this nationalization of truth. It can create consciousness about the moral and legal criteria of international conduct by which men and women can effectively criticize their own government. Far from being aloof from or incompatible with international peace research, national peace research should proceed within the framework of international peace research.

But the starting-point for peace research in any country will have to be the present situation. Since the historical evolution of each group has its own peculiarities, each group may have its own ways and possibilities of achieving peace. If peace research starts from the peculiarities of each nation, it can express itself in the specific national pattern of thought. The most difficult task in starting a peace research programme in any country is to decide the nature of the research to be undertaken. The performance of this task requires three important things: the identification of problems for research in the national context; the awareness of the extent to which those problems provide a link between national peace and international peace; and the conscious effort to further the peace research programme on the basis of cooperation among scholars all over the world. It is the first requirement that will form the subject matter of the present chapter. Since the other two requirements should serve as a guide to the selection of problems for peace research, they would be referred to only indirectly.

If the international character of peace research is borne in mind, then it should seem logical that no self-righteous attitude about any particular country being in a special position to contribute to peace research should be encouraged. Peace research deals with matters that affect the whole world and thus it is important to be informed of the situation in every part of the world. As such, every country is important in terms of its potentiality to contribute to peace research. After the attainment of independence by India under Gandhi's leadership, India was regarded for some years as a country placed in a special position to guide the world in achieving permanent peace. Now this attitude survives only in the minds of some neo-Gandhians within India only. Scholars returning from their visit abroad tell us in private conversations that nobody outside India seriously believes that there is any effective peace movement or peace research movement in this country. This image of India is not wholly unjustifiable either. Although there is in India a long tradition of pacifist philosophy in which it takes so much pride, no systematic effort has been made in India to rediscover the meaning and significance of that tradition in the context of the present problem of international peace. So much so that even on Gandhi scientific study has been possible not in India but elsewhere. It has been possible in the United States and also in small countries like Sweden and Norway.

I

This does not mean that India cannot make any contribution to peace research. What is intended is to underline the fact that the claim to India being in a special position to contribute to peace without an adequate effort involving purposeful research activity is nothing more than mere sentimentalism. Therefore, for any peace research programme in India, it is necessary to get over this type of sentimentalism. This is not to say, however, that no peace research can be started unless this sentimentalism is completely got over. In a sense, the progress of peace research and the abandonment of sentimentalism should go on simultaneously. For the scientific knowledge yielded by peace research will itself remove some of the sentimentalism which is alien to any science. On the other hand, the removal of sentimentalism will pave the way for a further and better kind of peace research.

The area in which sentimentalism has been a most serious obstacle in peace research in this country is research on Gandhi. Nonviolence has been preached and practised in all known periods of human history. But it is Gandhi that brought nonviolence to its latest phase. Obviously, therefore, a study of Gandhi should form a part of peace research Without giving the impression that India has a monopoly of Gandhi, it can be pointed out that research on Gandhi is perhaps easier in India than elsewhere. For one thing, it is easier for an Indian scholar to read Gandhi's mind in the background of Indian traditions and, for another, a number of persons with whom Gandhi had close association are still alive and a peace researcher can benefit from them. But what is easy has not been made possible. This is due partly to the lack of competence in social science and partly to the unstated belief that whatever can be known about Gandhi has been known. The second reason is even more important. For the knowledge about Gandhi, which is considered final, is not only not complete but also not wholly correct. At a popular level, Gandhi is known in India mainly as a political leader who tried to moralize politics. Scholars, on the other hand, have studied Gandhi's ideas mostly in terms of the extent to which they may be fitted in defined categories. Those who are called neo-

Gandhians consider it their duty to defend and eulogize whatever Gandhi might have said and have consequently earned for themselves the charge of "insincerity and religiosity". In India, the present state of knowledge about Gandhi, therefore, is full of sentimentalism which has no scientific basis and thus cannot be helpful in the furtherance of peace research. Gandhi himself was never wearied of reminding us that he did not claim any finality about the ideas he presented. His philosophy, if it can be called by that name, was the result of constant search after truth. This search after truth, as the first chapter would show, is the essence of science. It would, therefore, be not only un-Gandhian but also unscientific to accept the Gandhian ideas unquestioningly.

Research on Gandhi is relevant to peace because Gandhi presented elaborate theories of war and peace and he came to know those theories scientifically. Thus Gandhi has significance for peace research not only for the content of his philosophy but also for the nature of his method. However, the relevance of Gandhi's philosophy and method has to be examined in the context of the present problem of peace. Almost every age in human history has developed a philosophy of pacifism to deal with questions raised by the realities of power and violence in human politics. There have been two major schools of pacifism in the political thought of the twentieth century—Christian pacifism and Gandhian pacifism. Although these two philosophies are akin in many respects, they are sufficiently dissimilar in context and approach. The new philosophy of pacifism required today has a greater chance of being successfully reconstructed on the basis of Gandhian pacifism than on that of Christian pacifism, because Gandhi made experiments in the application of nonviolence in group life on a large scale. The period after Gandhi's death, however, posed some troublesome problems of modern politics to which Gandhi did not or could not give serious thought. One such problem is the introduction of nonviolence in all aspects of life on a world scale.

The most important field of study on Gandhi, therefore, is provided by the need to attempt to explore the possibility of rebuilding a Gandhian theory applicable to world society as a whole. Is it possible? If so, how? If not, why? The extent to which these questions are answerable will decide what relevance Gandhi has for research on peace. But the attempt to explore the possibility of a general Gandhian theory must be preceded by an attempt to isolate those pressing problems and issues to which Gandhi did not give much attention or which, even if Gandhi might have thought about them, have assumed new dimensions after Gandhi's death. Having isolated such problems and issues, an inquiry can be made as to what Gandhi would have held about those problems and issues or how and to what extent he would have modified his views about them in the context of changed circumstances. Care will have to be taken, however, to suggest modifications only in what Gandhi considered non-essentials because it was only in non-essentials that he was prepared for compromise. At a higher level, of course, one can also reinterpret Gandhi in order to examine whether the line drawn by him between essentials and non-essentials still holds good. This examination will obviously proceed in the light of the requirements of peace and it might suggest that certain things considered as essentials by Gandhi should now be counted among non-essentials and vice versa.

An investigation into Gandhian ideas in the perspective suggested by the above remarks can make a good beginning in peace research in India. This perspective has been clearly created by the need for the rediscovery of Gandhi. It is difficult to present any exhaustive list of subjects to be explored in this context. However, a broad indication may be given of a few possible areas in which research must be undertaken. Since the development of a science of peace depends upon the emergence of a general theory of war and peace, research on Gandhi should proceed with a view to finding out how far Gandhi is relevant to the reconstruction of such a general theory. An important dimension of this relevance is opened up by the question whether Gandhian ideas are valid to India only or to the whole world. It is a question of the relationship between Gandhi and India on the one hand and between Gandhi and the rest of the world on the other.

It is in this context that two fundamental questions arise demanding scientific inquiry. One, what is there in common between Gandhi and the world minus India?, and, two, what is the nature of the interest of the non-India world in Gandhi? Research done on the first question so far has only revealed that Gandhi was greatly "influenced" by non-Indian philosophers like Tolstoy, Ruskin, Thoreau, and by the Quakers. However, it appears to this writer that there are only some points of similarity (as there are points of dissimilarity also) between Gandhi and other thinkers and these points of similarity do not represent any substantial influence of theirs on Gandhi. Indeed Gandhi himself acknowledged the influence of Tolstoy, Ruskin, and Thoreau. But a study at a deeper level would show something different. In fact, Gandhi learnt very little from history. His method was empirical. If he approved of some of the ideas of western thinkers, it was just accidental and could hardly be called a part of the natural growth of a practical philosophy which Gandhi developed in his social milieu. If he liked some of the ideas of the west, it was only because they appeared to him to be in keeping with his own philosophy and not because they provided any basis for the development of his philosophy. But this does not mean that Gandhi ignored modern western society and its demands. His genuis lay in his capacity to use the traditional in the promotion of the novel. He reinterpreted tradition in such a way that revolutionary ideas, clothed in familiar expression, could be readily adopted and employed towards revolutionary ends. In this sense the development of Gandhian philosophy is syncretic. The traditional Indian and the modern western, both function in Gandhian philosophy. How the two streams merged and how Gandhi's creative leadership transformed elements from both to develop the technique of action is the most important part of Gandhian philosophy. For the technique of action is not only his most notable contribution but it is also the realm in which Gandhi has left the greatest impact on the west.

It will, therefore, be an interesting field of investigation to examine the nature of Gandhi's impact on the west in the field of nonviolent technique of resolving conflicts. This examination will cover two aspects: the nature of Gandhian technique itself and the nature of the current techniques that are being developed under the influence of Gandhi. In its totality the attempt should be to reconstruct effective peaceful techniques of action. Such a reconstruction would be possible only on the basis of a scientific study not only of those uses of nonviolence which were made in the west after Gandhi but also of those which were made before Gandhi emerged as the recognized theorizer and implementor of nonviolence. Research on Gandhi in the framework of peace research should aim at discovering not only his impact on succeeding generations but also the place that he occupied in the general tradition of pacifism.

There have been a number of instances during the nineteenth and twentieth centuries outside India of the use of nonviolent resistance by individuals and groups. Some of these instances are the nonviolent movement of Hungary in the middle of the nineteenth century under the leadership of Francis Deak, the prevention of a war between Norway and Sweden by the socialists of the two countries by nonviolent means in 1905, the heroic nonviolent struggle of the people of West Samoa during 1920-36, the nonviolent resistance of the Norwegians against the Quisling regime and the German occupying force during the Second World War, the passive resistance of the people of Finland during 1898-1917 against the Russian attempt to Russianize the country, the Egyptian passive resistance against England during 1919-22, and the passive resistance of the people of the Ruhr to the Belgian-French occupation in 1923.

Among the more recent instances may be counted the passive resistance of the people of Denmark to the Nazis in 1940, the Norwegian teachers' resistance in 1942, the South African Defy Unjust Laws Campaign in 1952, the strike at the Vorkuta prison camp by 2,50,000 political prisoners in the Soviet Union in 1953, the Japanese resistance against the construction of a United States Air Force base at Sunakawa, Japan, and the Montgomery bus boycott in the United States in 1955-56. Besides, the noviolent revolutionary approach has been manifest in a small form since about the year 1945 in various parts of the world including (apart from India) Hong Kong, Germany, the United States, and England.

A thorough study of the use of nonviolent means referred to above is called for. The use of nonviolent means in the cases cited above represents the practical level of nonviolence.

Thus the Anglo-American (or the western) interest in Gandhism is confined to nonviolent techniques of political resistance and the Gandhian techniques of resolving conflicts. But the view is sometimes expressed that the adoption of nonviolent techniques in the west has been an incomplete effect of Gandhi inasmuch as it is shorn of the ethical and religious considerations as also of the view of an ideal society, all of which are the essentials of Gandhian philosophy. That the west has taken only certain aspects of Gandhism for use as effective techniques is, of course, true. But to call it a distortion of Gandhism would perhaps be too much. Peace research is interested in a meaningful reconstruction of peaceful techniques. And in any reconstruction the question of distortion should not arise. Gandhi's message after all is universal. Gandhi repeatedly reminded us that his message and methods are, in their essentials, for the whole world. In fact, the technique aspect of Gandhism is the most important part because the end itself evolves, as Gandhi never wearied of reminding us, out of the constant practice of, and adherence to, the right means. Therefore, it is not important in what kind of society the Gandhian technique is practised. Means are of primary consideration. Everything else is subordinate.

If this line of reasoning is accepted, then it would not be proper to say that the mere adoption of the nonviolent technique, taking it out of the total philosophical system of Gandhi, would be a distortion of Gandhism. Such a view seems to presume that the nonviolent technique developed and practised by Gandhi can have relevance and be successful only when and if the people who practise it believe in all the principles of Gandhi regarding cosmology, the nature of man, the individual and society and even ethical and metaphysical principles. But the Khudai Khidmatgar movement led by Khan Abdul Ghaffar Khan (the Frontier Gandhi) in the North West Frontier Province of undivided India was based on the principle of nonviolence, although the Moslem Pathans are well known as brave warriors trained in the use of arms and unfamiliar with a tradition of philosophy enjoining nonviolence. Yet the movement was as successful as in predominantly Hindu India. It would, therefore, be an interesting study to enquire whether a faith in the total philosophical system of Gandhi and the

Hindu milieu in which Gandhi mostly worked are necessary for the acceptance and application of the Gandhian technique.

The Gandhian technique is not bound in time and space. However, the idea is not that a set blueprint of a nonviolent technique can succeed anywhere and at any time. Surely, it has got to be altered here and there to suit the change in time and environment. The problem for research is whether the Gandhian technique, even with suitable modifications, will succeed. This question is pertinent in the context of any non-Hindu society. Therefore, an examination of this question is required at a general and theoretical plane, without confining it to the west.

In revising the Gandhian technique of nonviolence, care is to be taken with regard to the long-term effect of the nonviolent technique. Focus is also to be given to the conditions contributing to the emergence of nonviolence as an adequate functional substitute for violence. These are the problems of research which even writers like Irving Janis and Daniel Katz, who have done quite commendable work in the field, have not taken up seriously. Peace research in India can fill this gap. This gap will be filled if the Gandhian technique of nonviolence is systematized as a sound technique of resolving intragroup and intergroup conflicts. As Gandhi always insisted on the constant practice of truth and on the permanent readiness to learn from every new truth as it emerges, this systematization will not only be quite in tune with the Gandhian method but also facilitate both a fuller appreciation of Gandhism itself and a clear understanding of what prospects the Gandhian technique offers of being successful in the present circumstances.

Whatever has been suggested above does not exhaust the scope of research on Gandhi, however. It only indicates some broad areas in which research may be undertaken. The progress of research in these areas may eventually open up new avenues for research on Gandhi.

II

In any case, the question of Gandhi's current relevance must be examined at two levels: the relevance to the world and the relevance to India. What can be the possibilities of research at the first level was pointed out in the first section. But at the second level, one has to take note of another important problem. This problem is to identify the sources of threat to peace within the Indian society. In other words, one has to locate the specific problems that are likely to create serious tensions in the country. It is only by locating such problems that we can find out whether Gandhi can be relevant in solving those problems and, if so, to what extent. An initial task connected with the development of a peace research programme in India, therefore, will be to give a careful thought to the question of identifying the problems that must be immediately taken up for research. This is not to say, however, that there is no knowledge available about those problems or that no research has been done on those problems. This is only to say that there may be several problems which either are not known or have not been broached by the peace research approach. Thus peace research in India will be concerned not only with new problems but also with old ones.

It is not possible for an individual to present any comprehensive list of problems of peace research in India. Such a list can be prepared only by some sort of a national committee consisting of persons with peace attitudes. Nor is it possible to have a ready-made list of research problems before a peace research programme begins. It is the submission of this writer that the actual scope of peace research in India will unfold itself as and when peace research proceeds. However, a reference might be made to certain broad areas of inquiry relevant to peace research. Such areas have to be identified in reference to India's current problems, both in the domestic and in the international field. The emphasis on *current problems* is on account of the fact that peace research, as argued in the first chapter, is concerned with specific problems. And problems have relevance mainly in the present. Thus peace research, being a continuous process, deals with those problems which may pose a threat to peace at a given time. On the basis of this criterion, one can find problems belonging to both the domestic and the international sphere as relevant to peace research.

The problem-oriented character of peace research, which

was emphasized in the first chapter, is significant in the context of possibilities of peace research in India also. E.H. Carr observed long ago (in a book cited in the third chapter) that peace is a by-product of the search for something else and that peace cannot be pursued as a goal directly. This observation applies to peace research not only in the international context but also in the national context. When Carr talks of "something else", his reference is to the need for establishing some goal whose pursuance results in peace.

This writer ventures to submit that the establishment of such a goal is a difficult task. One can at best proceed with a general proposition that members of a society must seek their objectives with peaceful methods. Thus peace will prevail in India if the demands of the various sections of its people are met by peaceful methods. The initial task of peace research in India, therefore, is to suggest the legitimate demands of the people and the peaceful means to their fulfilment. In performing this task, peace research has to discover not only those common demands that are significant to all sections of people but also those that are likely to lead to any kind of conflict among people. In a sense, the latter category of demands is more important than the former. For it is through an identification of the latter category of demands that peace research can point out sources of conflict and suggest peaceful ways of resolving it. In both the cases, peace research will be concerned with producing knowledge. This knowledge can then be utilized in tackling those problems that threaten peace.

However, this knowledge can be produced by research on specific problems. It is often assumed that peace is the result of integrated behaviour, based on sentiments of solidarity and concern for the common good among the members of a society. In India also, emphasis has been laid on national integration for many years. To achieve the "objective" of national integration, conferences have been held, appeals have been made, and reports have been submitted. But what is often forgotten is the fact that national integration, like peace, is not an end which can be pursued for its own sake. Like peace, national integration is a by-product of something else. It would not be correct to say that peace requires only integrated behaviour or that integrated behaviour necessarily results in peace. In fact, joint pursuit of common ends by peaceful means leads to integrated behaviour and to the attainment of peace. Thus both integration and peace are the results or by-products of peaceful efforts to achieve well-defined objectives. Peace research in India, therefore, can take up the problem of interrelationship between peace and national integration. It should be remembered that the essential feature of this interrelationship is that behaviours, whether similar or different, must always complement each other towards the ultimate end.

This suggests that an integrated behaviour is end-oriented. As such, there must be a clearly defined end for the attainment of which behaviours of men can or should be integrated. It may be that the ultimate end requires different kinds of activities. But the justness or otherwise of such activities will be decided by referring them to the requirements of the overall objective. Thus the successful integration for peace depends upon the proper formulation of the nature of the end.

The problem of interrelationship between integration and peace in India arises mainly because India is one of those heterogenous societies whose members pursue a multiplicity of goals. Some of these goals may be unrelated to each other and at times may even be in conflict among themselves. There is, therefore, need for preventing the use of violence that may be made to deal with the situation resulting from the incompatibility of interests. Another important area of peace research in India is, then, provided by this need. Research undertaken to fulfil this need will point out the sources of the incompatibility of interests on the one hand and suggest ways of resolving the incompatibility by peaceful methods on the other. The performance of both these tasks, however, will be preceded by the formulation of the nature of the overall end.

The only overall end on which people generally agree is the maintenance of the nation itself or, in other words, the security of the nation. But there can be differences of opinion as to how the overall end can be achieved. Every citizen can interpret the requirements of this end in the light of his own needs and expectations. This puts a serious limitation on the possibility of integration of behaviour. One often finds in India that there are high demands for the satisfaction of particular needs. But there is hardly any real agreement on how to achieve the ultimate end, namely the sense of unity and nationhood. What peace research has to do is not merely to state that the continued peaceful existence of India's unity is the overall objective (for that is already a part of common awareness), but to stress that the fulfilment of the various demands and expectations is itself possible only within the framework of the overall objective. In pointing out the sources of the incompatibility of interests, therefore, reference will have to be made to the ultimate end.

In this context, two problems for research can be taken up. One will be concerned with the relationship between the incompatibility of interests and the overall objective and the other with the peaceful methods of the resolution of the incompatibility and the preservation of the overall objective. Research on these problems must start with the assumption that the preservation of the overall objective is to a large extent the problem of resolving the incompatibility of interests. For, at times, the incompatibility may be so serious as to frustrate the common objective altogether. In addition to pointing out the sources of the incompatibility of interests, therefore, peace research can also isolate the less serious sources from the more serious ones.

Since peace research is primarily concerned with the production of knowledge (as argued in the first chapter), it will not be sufficient if peace research in India only points out the sources of incompatibility or conflict and distinguishes the less serious sources from the more serious ones. It will have to go further and discover the causes and suggest remedies. For it is only by doing so that it can produce scientific knowledge about what threatens peace in India and what should be done to guard against the threat.

That peace in India is currently threatened is obvious. The recent few years, especially those after Nehru's death, have shown not only the magnitude of problems with which India is faced but also the ever-growing readiness of many sections of Indian people to resort to the use of violence. It would be a rewarding study if the causes of this readiness to use violence are analysed. The problem can be examined both from a psychological and from a realistic point of view.

At the realistic level, two aspects are important. One is

that in a large society like India consisting of different groups, there is always a situation in which the same persons are competitors in some roles and collaborators in others. Such a characteristic situation imposes limits on both hostility and friendship among men. Thus it is not possible that there is absolutely no use or manifestation of violence in a society which is, or seeks to be, peaceful. Every society has some tolerance of the use of violence. But the extent of this tolerance should be determined in accordance with whether the use of violence threatens the overall objective. Thus an important function of peace research is to draw a line of demarcation between one use of violence that can be tolerated and the other use of violence that threatens the continued peaceful existence of a society. Peace research can produce knowledge about how to keep the use of violence at the minimum.

The other important aspect of the realistic approach to the problem of violence is derived from the problem-oriented character of peace research. For scientific knowledge can be produced only through research on concrete problems.

III

One of the most urgent problems facing India is population control. Research in demography has shown that world population stood somewhere between 300 and 400 million in the year about 1600. It took about two hundred years for this figure to double up. Thus at the end of the eighteenth century world population was about 800 million which rose up to about 1500 million in only one hundred years, that is, by the beginning of the twentieth century. The further doubling up process took only about sixty years, with the result that world population touched the point of 3000 million by the 1960s. It is feared that if the present rate of the growth of population continues for six hundred years, the available land space of the world would be just sufficient for all men to stand shoulder to shoulder. The problem of population control may be taken up at the international level. But it should also be taken up at the national level. That India is one of the most overpopulated countries is everybody's knowledge But it is doubtful whether a scientific study has been made of the problems of peace indicated by this knowledge. As such, an important problem relevant to peace research in India is population control. Research on this problem must be based on a two-dimensional approach, inasmuch as it must adopt the techniques of the science of demography on the one hand and those of sociology on the other. The techniques of demography will help in an analysis of the causes of population growth, whereas those of sociology will help the researcher in establishing a relationship between population and peace. In its totality, the attempt must be to explain how overpopulation produces tension and threatens peace. Peace research may not necessarily suggest practical ways of population control. It will have achieved its objective if only it is able to establish the link between peace and population. For by doing so, it will have created the awareness that population control is as important for the welfare of India as socialism, non-alignment, or internationalism could be.

The problem of population is intimately connected with the problem of food. Surely, it should be obvious that if genuine peace is to be achieved and preserved, there should be enough for men, women, and children to eat. There can be several ways of tackling the problem of food shortage with which India is confronted. Population control is one of them and the use of improved methods of agriculture may be another. But ultimately India's problem of food has to be looked upon as a part of the international problem of food. In the San Francisco Conference, the only problems discussd were problems of power. The basic problem of mankind, that of food, was relegated to an obscure international committee on agriculture. It is a fashion to believe that Malthus was wrong because he did not foresee that improved methods of transport could transfer food surpluses from one area to another area where there is shortage. This, however, is not the whole truth. For one thing, such a transfer of food supplies cannot be possible during wartime or during the time when the relations between the countries falling within the surplus area and those falling within the shortage area are not cordial; and, for another, even food supplies under present conditions are used as weapons in the game of power. These two factors limit the advantages of an international solution of the food problem. But it is the submission of this writer that the evil effect of these factors can perhaps be mitigated, at least partially, if the food problem is taken up internationally but in a way different from the way in which it is being dealt with now. At present, it is being tackled mainly at the bilateral level. The international agencies connected indirectly with this problem are concerned either with improving methods of agriculture or with providing relief to certain areas stricken by acute food crisis. What is required is a regular transfer of food from surplus areas to areas of shortage under the supervision and control of international organization. This transfer must be as important a primary responsibility of the United Nations as the maintenance of international peace and security. It is at this point that internationally organized peace researchers might contribute to the cause of peace by pointing out the potentialities of international organization in the realm of the food problem and by suggesting that an essential element of international cooperation is the willingness of countries with surplus food to part with it for the sake of those who need it. This is essentially the function of international peace research. But national peace research in India can also contribute to international peace research in this context. A beginning in this direction might be made by starting a research project on the motives of those countries that have given food aid to India. An understanding of the motives might enable the policy-makers of this country to bring some realism to bear on their policies and discover a basis on which food supplies from surplus areas might be available on a permanent footing. This is not to suggest that the goal of self-sufficiency in food should be abandoned. But so long as self-sufficiency is not achieved, dependence on food supplies from other countries is unavoidable. Peace research should, therefore, take up the problem of the scarcity of food as seriously as the problem of overpopulation. For both of them constitute a potential threat to peace. Thus, in the context of the Indian situation, peace research can be defined, though only in a limited sense, as the intellectual effort to explain how overpopulation and food shortage pose a threat to the preservation of peace in India and to recommend how best the threat can be averted.

There is yet another area in which peace research can do

fruitful work in India. This area is provided by the changing political situation in the country. The results of the Fourth General Election are significant in more than one ways. First, they show the declining confidence of people in the Congress; secondly, they indicate the growing political maturity of the Indian electorate; and thirdly, they have created a state of transition for Indian politics. This three-dimensional significance of the Fourth General Election provides scope for a number of peace research projects. The third aspect, however, is more important than the first and the second. Because an analysis of the factors responsible for the declining confidence in the Congress may be directly relevant only to the Congress Party, whereas a study of the growing political maturity may be purely of a historical interest. These two aspects can be relevant to peace research only indirectly and only in so far as they help in the study of the transitional situation in terms of its potential danger to India's peace and stability. The first important task of peace research in this matter is, therefore, to examine the nature of the transition created by the Fourth Election. The focus of this examination will be on the possibility of the emergence of an alternative political party as a substitute for the Congress Party through constitutional methods. The results of the Fourth General Election have shown a reduction in the Congress majority at the Centre and the failure of the Congress Party to command absolute majority in several States. But they have not shown an absolute majority for any other single party (except the Dravida Munnetra Kazhagam in Madras). The inevitable consequence of all this will be that difficulties will be encountered in the smooth functioning of the government at the Centre where the Congress has a rather slender majority and in those States where coalition governments have been set up. To analyse the nature of such difficulties is one of the aspects of the examination of the transition created in Indian politics after the 1967 elections. For example, it would be worth while to study the relationship between the Centre and the States with non-Congress governments. Another problem for research can be the relationship between the government and the opposition both at the Centre and at the State levels. It would also be an interesting study to compare the performance of the Congress Party where it is in power on the one hand and where it is in opposition on the other. Such a comparative study can also be made about other important political parties like the Swatantra Party, the Bharatiya Jana Sangh, the Communist Party, and the Dravida Munnetra Kazhagam. The basic point of inquiry behind this type of studies would be whether the various political parties maintain uniformity of policy and attitude without being influenced by the consideration of being in or out of power.

But the uniformity of policy and attitude of a political party is essentially a matter of finding out a role for that party itself. In trying to inquire whether such a uniformity exists, peace research will therefore be doing nothing else than investigating whether the major political parties of India are aware of the role that they are to play in the social and political life of the country. Peace research must, then, point out which party has a role to perform and what that role is. In so doing, peace research may also suggest what role should be played by which political party. Thus peace research will be concerned not merely with defining the role of those political parties which may have a role but also with assigning a role to those parties which may not have any. The definition and the assigning of role will, however, be on the basis of the overall requirements of peace and stability. Since these requirements may vary from time to time, it is necessary to redefine and reassign the role in accordance with new requirements. In other words, the task of peace research in this regard is continuous.

There are two other specific problems of research that can be undertaken in this context. How far have the political parties of India been transforming themselves in terms of policies and behaviour according to changing conditions? What are the prospects of the emergence of a bi-party system in India? The first question is related to an analysis of the past and the second to that of the future. But both of them are interconnected among themselves. For trends discernible from the past can also serve as indicators for the future. Research on the first question can proceed with a comparative study of the election manifestos of the various political parties. This comparative study will have two dimensions: one relating to a comparison of the various election manifestos of each single party and the other relating to a comparison between the manifestos of various parties. The former can be called the intra-party comparison and the latter the inter-manifesto comparison. The results of this study can then be utilized as a basis for investigation into the second question, namely the possibility of the emergence of a bi-party system in India. The point of direct inquiry in this connexion would be which party or a combination of parties might emerge as the second alternative party. Peace research may also examine the merits and demerits of the case for a national government put by Chakravarti Rajagopalachari, Jayaprakash Narayan, and others.

IV

In the field of international relations also, peace research can undertake several projects in which India's interests are involved. In particular, these projects should be related to India's relations with China and Pakistan.

A study of Sino-Indian relations provides a lesson and an explanation. The lesson is that it is not always easy to achieve success in new experiments in international relations and the explanation is that the various phases in relations between India and China have been just the stages of the transformation of a latent into an overt conflict. The lesson and the explanation can facilitate a reappraisal of Sino-Indian relations.

This reappraisal starts with the assumption that almost all relationships emerging from human interaction contain aspects that are inherently conflictual and that even in most hostile relationships there is a trace of cooperation. Resolution or elimination of conflicts requires the widening of the area of cooperation and lessening of the area of conflictual aspects. If this is borne in mind, then it would explain for itself why a study of Sino-Indian relations should start from the very time when actual interaction between free India and China began. The fact which made an inherent conflict possible between India and China at that time was the existence of two countries with apparently incompatible interests, aims, values, and beliefs. It was, in other words, a latent conflict which becomes an overt conflict only when both the parties concerned decide to resolve it by a behaviour that is likewise incompatible or mutually injurious. But there are other ways also of resolving conflicts. One of them is to deal with the incompatibles at a higher plane at which they appear to be compatible or less incompatible so that it restrains the parties concerned from adopting the course of mutually injurious behaviour. That is exactly what Nehru tried to do in the initial phases of India's relations with China. Nehru's repeated emphasis on not to think of Sino-Indian relations in terms of communism and anti-communism is an indication of his anxiety to prevent the latent conflict from developing into an overt conflict. Therefore, all that India did to end the isolation of China, to vindicate its claim to Taiwan, and to support it on various other issues was to bring home the impression to the Chinese that the fact that India and China had two different systems would not be allowed to affect the relations of the two countries.

It is not very easy to say with any degree of certainty how far China understood or appreciated this way of preventing the transformation of conflict. But its response was clearly not very encouraging. For the resolution of conflict depends upon an adequate communication system between the parties in the pattern of their external behaviour. Whatever may have been the determinants of Chinese attitudes and actions, their action in Tibet in 1950 and their critical statements about India in that year were a primary factor in the failure of India's initiative for friendship with China. From the point of view of world public opinion in general the dominant motive behind all actions of the Communist Chinese regime during early years—like the conquest of Tibet, the intervention in the Korean War, and the support for the Viet Minh in Indochina—was communism. By looking at international issues with the assumptions of communism and anti-communism, China put a brake on India's efforts for a new experiment in international relations and earned for India many uncomplimentary remarks including the one that India's China policy was an adventurism in foreign affairs. The post-1950 period was an a period in which the importance of the avoidance of conflict by not stressing the incompatibles was realized. It would appear, then, that but for the rigorous pursuit of Communist policies, China would have got the United Nations seat and Formosa in 1950. However, Sino-Indian relations during the earlier period cannot be defined in clear terms. They connot be described as friendly because of China's hostile attitude, nor as hostile because of India's effort to win Chinese friendship, nor even as conflictual by which is meant that relationship in which each party perceives the interests of the other to be incompatible with its own and the behaviour of the other party as injurious or potentially injurious. This is what India seems to have tried to avoid from the very beginning. It would thus not be wrong to say that India's relations with China in the initial phases were of a unique character.

It is suggested, therefore, that a study of Sino-Indian relations may be made with the help of sociological theories of transformation of conflict. However, the absence of China's response to India's initiative of what has been called a new experiment in international relations should not give the impression that Sino-Indian relations have always been governed by ideological differences. As years went by, there was indeed a relaxation in the Chinese attitude which facilitated the formulation of a basis for mutual intimacy between India and China reaching its high water-mark at Bandung and in Panchasheela. But this relaxation was made by China and treated by India at a rather superficial level. For, whereas there was an increase in cooperation between India and China, the two countries did not succeed in evolving an abiding basis for a permanent friendship based upon that relaxation. During the period which appeared to the world to be a period of honeymoon between India and China, the border question was left undealt with and was not touched seriously by either of the countries in their discussions held at various levels. The very fact that this question was postponed shows that this was an incompatible aspect of Sino-Indian relations. Of course, the border question existed even before. But it was perceived as being an incompatible aspect only later and it is the perception, not the existence, of an incompatible aspect that determines whether a relation is conflictual or not. It would, therefore, not be incorrect to say that Sino-Indian relations during the later period and down to the beginning of the year 1957 which were regarded as apparently cordial and friendly were worse in the later period than in the earlier period, because in the earlier period there was no mutual perception of the incompatible aspect. Not only does this perception, called awareness in common parlance, explain Sino-Indian relations in their most crucial period but it is also the strongest defence which the Government of India can put up against all criticism of negligence of "the growing Chinese menace to India".

During the period following the year 1957, the range of the incompatible aspect of Sino-Indian relations rapidly widened and with that its perception became clearer. The "minor border incidents", the controversy about maps in the form of Nehru's objections and Chou En-lai's evasive answers, and various other developments all seem to lend weight to this contention. There are people who assume that India annoyed China by taking steps for the revivalism of Buddhism in India in 1956, that Chou En-lai expected a part of Kashmir's territory in case of a plebiscite there (based upon Suhrawardy's suggestion that the Buddhists of Kashmir would vote for Tibet in case of a plebiscite in Kashmir), and that there started a competition between India and China for economic development. All these assumptions, though far-fetched in analysis, can appear to have at least a modicum of truth if viewed in the light of the observation made above.

Even during the conflictual stage of Sino-Indian relations, an attempt to avoid the transformation of conflict is discernible at least in Indian diplomacy. Its continued pleading for a UN seat for China and its supposed satisfaction with the vague replies of China to its objections to Chinese maps were nothing but an expression of the desire to narrow the area of conflict and widen that of cooperation. It is only in terms of this desire that one can explain Nehru's oft-repeated concern that we should avoid doing or saying anything which might hurt Chinese national prestige and honour.

But this could not prevent the transformation of the latent conflict into an overt conflict. During the transformation, another process was at work and it reached its climax when the Chinese invasion took place. This process was the transformation of the latent conflict into a non-identified conflict which calls for the existence of mutually perceived incompatible aims that are perceived to reside in one or a few tangible areas of dispute. The resolution of these tangible disputes constitutes the elimination of conflict. In the case of Sino-

Indian relations, the tangible dispute was obviously the border dispute which began with "minor border incidents". Whatever the reason, the resolution of this tangible dispute was not possible, in spite of pronounced faith of both India and China in negotiations. The best time for the resolution of this dispute was when this faith was at its peak. The fact that India offered negotiations and China responded favourably, at least openly, and the further fact that even then it could not solve what has been called the tangible dispute suggest that there was a break somewhere in the communication between the two countries. When, where, and in which manner did this break come about is extremely difficult to say unless one goes through the secret files. For the present purpose, however, it is sufficient to remember that the non-resolution of the tangible dispute by a compatible method, i.e., negotiations, led to two unhappy developments in Sino-Indian relations. One was the narrowing of what is called the threshold of tolerance or, to borrow a concept from Chester Bernard, the zone of indifference, and the other was the gradual force of circumstances compelling a shift of attention from the compatible to the incompatible means of settling the dispute. Whether these two developments were the result of the growing power of both India and China or of the compulsions of international politics does not help us much in the present undertaking. What is important is that they helped the process of the transformation of the latent conflict into an overt conflict.

The last few years of Sino-Indian relations hastened this process which ultimately developed into an open conflict between India and China in October 1962, when India decided to strike back because an overt conflict exists only at a point where the victim of initiatory and incompatible action strikes back. Once a conflict of this type starts it has a tendency to develop into an identified conflict, as distinguished from a non-identified conflict referred to earlier, which is identified with the self of a state and which may exist even in the absence of tangible disputes. Thus an identified conflict often leaves a residual perception of conflict even after the tangible dispute has been solved. The conflict in which India and China are involved today is fast assuming the character of an identified conflict. It is quite likely, therefore, that even after the settlement of the border problem, the residual perception of conflict might give rise to fresh tangible disputes between India and China and thus make the Sino-Indian conflict a more permanent phenomenon in international affairs.

The avoidance of the emergence of disputes is the concern of peace researchers. A study of Sino-Indian relations may, therefore, be undertaken along the lines suggested above. This study will focus the causes of conflict between India and China and the possible ways in which the relations between the two countries could be improved. It may also be pointed out here that an essential requirement for the possible improvement in Sino-Indian relations is the creation of the public opinion needed for it. How to meet this requirement can also be a suitable subject for peace research.

A study of Indo-Pakistani relations may also be made almost along the same lines. This study should proceed with the recognition of the fact that the present state of Indo-Pakistani relations is marked by a great deal of mutual fear and suspicion and hostility. The causes of this state of relations between India and Pakistan have been analysed rather sufficiently both in India and in other countries. Whereas it is necessary to have a balanced view of these causes as also of the arguments and counterarguments put forth by India and Pakistan in support of their stands towards each other, it is not of much significance from the point of view of peace research. For peace research goes further from discovering the causes of conflict and suggests methods of its resolution. In the case of Indo-Pakistani relations, therefore, peace research should try to point out how the causes of conflict can be avoided.

It is suggested that the experiment made by Nehru in the prevention of the crystallization of India's conflict with China may be made in the case of Indo-Pakistani relations, though in a slightly different form. The essential difference between the case of China and that of Pakistan is that when Nehru made the experiment, the conflict between India and China was only inherent and non-identified, whereas the conflict between India and Pakistan is not only overt but also identified. Therefore, it is necessary that the overt and identified character of the Indo-Pakistani conflict is borne in mind when suggestions are made for the resolution of the conflict. In approaching the problem of Indo-Pakistani relations from the peace research angle, the following appear to be relevant. One, that the objective of the study is the normalization of relations between India and Pakistan; two, that no political solution can be found to the problems between India and Pakistan; and three, that peaceful relations between the two countries are possible. All the three things are connected with the basic assumption that peace between India and Pakistan is a desirable goal. Peace research, which is gradually becoming a value science, will take up the problem of Indo-Pakistani relations with a view to finding out ways and means for the fulfilment of the value of peace between the two countries. In doing so, peace research will first of all suggest ways of transforming the identified conflict between India and Pakistan into a non-identified one and then point out how the conflict can be resolved peacefully.

The performance of this task by peace research will be preceded by a clear establishment of the postulate that India and Pakistan have certain common interests which are more important than the issues on which they find their views irreconcilable. This itself is a problem of change of attitude in both India and Pakistan. But the change of attitude cannot be brought about merely by pious hopes and wishful thinking. Peace research will have to suggest how the change of attitude can be effected.

There is a possibility that if India and Pakistan work together in the field of common interest, they might undergo a change of attitude. But what the field of common interest is, is a problem for research. It will, therefore, be worth while to examine the prospects of Indo-Pakistani cooperation in areas of common interest on the one hand and to identify what these areas of common interest could be. Although one can know the full nature of these areas only after systematic research, one can tentatively think of two of these areas. One is the area of economic cooperation between India and Pakistan and the other is that of political cooperation between them for keeping outside influence out of the Indo-Pakistani subcontinent. If the significance of the two areas of cooperation is realized by India and Pakistan and if cooperation in these areas goes ahead, it might bring about the desired change of attitude.

Besides, a study of the attitude of India to Pakistan and of Pakistan to India would also be fruitful. This study can be made in two parts: one dealing with the official attitude and the other dealing with the non-official attitude. In a sense, the non-official attitude is more important than the official attitude. For the latter is often determined by the former. Peace research can suggest how the present anti-Pakistani public opinion in India can change. In this context, it would be necessary to think of the role which political parties and important individuals can play in building the correct image of Pakistan in India and of India in Pakistan and in creating the opinion that the future of India and Pakistan lies in their working together for peace and welfare of both of them. It is necessary because neither the Government of India nor the Government of Pakistan can change their policies towards each other without an adequate support or demand for it by public opinion at home.

In studying problems of this nature, peace research can utilize the latest theories of conflict. Mention may be made here of the various models built by scholars like Charles Osgood, Thomas Schelling, Anatol Rapoport, and Joseph Nogee. These and various other writers have emphasized the fact that international disputes today cannot be solved by the use of force and that we should strengthen the instrument of negotiation. Various models have been built to study various crisis situations in international relations. But no attempt has so far been made to build or apply any model in the case of Indo-Pakistani relations. This can now be done under a peace research programme. A beginning can be made in this field by studying the processes of decision-making both in India and in Pakistan. This study will primarily be concerned with those foreign policy decisions that have a direct or indirect bearing on Pakistan's policy towards India and on India's policy towards Pakistan.

A special mention may be made of the need for a study of the problem of Kashmir. The rigidity of attitude of India and Pakistan on Kashmir is well-known. Whether it is possible to achieve some solution of the problem in spite of the rigidity of attitude is the question that can be taken up by peace research. The suggestions made by Jayaprakash Narayan may provide the basis in this connexion. Jayaprakash Narayan's suggestion is based upon the faith that a solution of the Kashmir problem is possible even without de-accession or the division of Kashmir. This possibility, according to Narayan, can be brought about by building up the will of the Kashmiris in support of Kashmir's continuance as a part of India. Narayan also suggests that the status of Kashmir need not necessarily be the same as that of other States of the Indian federation. He holds that if India is able to convince world public opinion that Kashmiris want to be with India, the Kashmir problem will cease to exist and that Pakistan's demand for a plebiscite in Kashmir will then have no meaning. Jayaprakash Narayan's scheme raises several questions that should be taken up by peace research. What is the way to discover the will of the people of Kashmir? What special status can reasonably be conceived of for the State of Jammu and Kashmir? How can the will of the Kashmiris be built in favour of India? These questions are all very important and research on them is likely to yield fruitful results. Besides, peace research can also start a research project dealing with the question of plebiscite. This project will be concerned with the meaning and relevance of plebiscite in international history. This project will make mainly a historical study of the various cases in which plebiscite was used for resolving international conflicts. This historical study may reveal what the conditions are under which plebiscite is relevant and what the conditions are under which it is not.

Another project on Kashmir may devote itself to the preparation of an inventory of the various solutions of the Kashmir problem that have been suggested so far by various non-official agencies and private individuals. The preparation of this inventory may then be followed by an examination of the merits and demerits of the various proposed solutions of the Kashmir problem.

V

The foregoing remarks would suggest that there is a large scope for peace research in India. Therefore, the question to which we should now address ourselves is how a beginning can be made in this regard. At present, there is no centre in this country which is devoted to peace research. The establishment of a peace research centre, therefore, seems to be an immediate necessity. It is not necessary that this centre should be started immediately as an independent and autonomous research institution. For that is neither possible nor desirable. The proposed peace reasearch centre should emerge as the result of gradual intensification of research for peace. To begin with, the Gandhian Institute of Studies, Varanasi, or the Indian School of International Studies, New Delhi, can establish a peace research unit within the existing framework of it research programme. The reason for a special mention of these two institutions is the fact that the former has already given indication of its interest in peace research and the latter is devoted to research in the field of international relations, an area which is so very relevant to peace research.

A peace research unit will be concerned in the beginning with preparing the ground for the development of a peace research programme in India. A number of steps might be suggested towards the development of this programme. First, a scholar should be asked to visit important institutions in the world. The institutions to be visited should be carefully selected; and the selection can be made on the basis of a twofold criterion: those institutions that are directly engaged in peace research and those that are directly concerned with other disciplines but that have at least a part of the programme based on peace research orientation. A visit to these institutions will be helpful in the development of peace research in several ways. For one thing it will enable the visiting scholar to acquire a first-hand knowledge of the way in which peace research is being conducted in other countries and, for another, it will provide an opportunity for a personal discussion of the possibility of foreign scholars cooperating with Indian scholars in the development of peace research in this country. Further, the suggested visit abroad may also be utilized in the collection of relevant material for a library on peace research.

The question of building a library on peace research is important. For no peace research programme can be meaningful without an adequate library. The second step necessary for starting peace research in India, therefore, is to make a beginning in the development of a library on peace research. At the initial stage, a comprehensive list of publications may be prepared. This list will contain a much larger number of items than those included in the third chapter dealing with a survey of recent peace studies. For that survey is selective, not exhaustive. Its purpose is only to introduce to the reader the major trends in peace research, not to present a complete list of items that could guide in building a library on the subject. The preparation of the list would be quite a job in itself and the list prepared may still not be really exhaustive. An exhaustive list can possibly be made only when advice is available of a scholar who has visited important centres of peace research in the world. But so long as such advice is not available, a tentative list can be prepared from the sources available in India. The most important source is the *International Peace Research Newsletter,* published every three months, which contains rich information about the progress of peace research in various parts of the world. Efforts may be made to acquire the material about which information is available from the *Newsletter*.

A second step in the direction of starting peace research in India might be taken by undertaking some of the research projects suggested earlier. These projects can be undertaken in universities and research centres in the country. Departments of history, political science, sociology, and international relations can certainly give a lead. To begin with, these departments can at least give a peace orientation to their research programme. In their teaching programme also, they can include a short course on peace research. The University of Mysore is planning to start a separate peace research section. But in other universities, peace research can be given a modest beginning even within the existing framework of social science departments.

CHAPTER THREE

Recent Studies in Peace Research

As the first chapter would show, an important feature of world politics in the mid-twentieth century is the growing concern for peace. This concern has also been reflected in the past whenever the world was faced with a crisis. But in view of the all-destructive character of nuclear weapons, the concern for peace has acquired added significance. For if a nuclear war breaks out, it would mean total annihilation. It is the realization of this potential threat to human survival that has led responsible people from all walks of life to think of ways and means by which war could be avoided and peace could be maintained. Finding out such ways and means is in brief the purpose of peace research. Efforts to curb the incidence of war were made before the Second World War also. But what distinguishes the current efforts from the past efforts is the fact that emphasis is laid today on developing such peaceful techniques which replace force as a method of resolving international conflicts and thus make peace a stable phenomenon. This itself is a complicated problem inasmuch it involves a correct appraisal of causes of war and conditions of peace which again is rendered difficult on account of growing complexities of life. Therefore, those who are engaged in peace research have had to adopt a multi-dimensional approach and hence anything may fall within the scope of their endeavours. Thus subjects like disarmament and arms control, conflict resolution, nonviolent movements, and international organization are all relevant to peace research.

An attempt will be made in this chapter to make a critical assessment of select publications on peace research. But since peace research is too wide a field to permit its definitive identification, a survey of this kind has to be more or less arbitrary in the selection of items to be included in it. Further, an attempt has been made here to choose only recent publications, preferably those of 1960s. If some old publications have been included, it is so only because of their exceptional usefulness. One such publication is *Research for Peace Essays*[1]. It is the collection of the three best essays written by Quincy Wright, W.F. Cottrell, and Ch. Boasson for a prize contest organized by the Institute for Social Research, Oslo. These essays examine the relevance of research to peace from various points of view. This collection of essays is indicative of the existence of numerous complex problems involved in defining peace research rather than of the discovery of an appropriate definition as such.

MEANING OF PEACE RESEARCH

Undoubtedly there are difficulties in defining the field of peace research. Nevertheless, scholars working in the field have made attempts to define peace research. One such attempt is "A Critical Definition of Peace Research"[2] by Johan Galtung who means by peace research that which is directed towards the understanding of conditions that contribute to the prevention of international and intergroup violence as also to the furtherance of harmonious and creative relations among nations and peoples. According to Galtung, peace research has two broad divisions: conflict research and peace initiatives. Research in these two fields is, broadly speaking, peace research. But peace being the concern of everyone on earth, peace research can be useful only when it is universal in its methodology and takes help from all relevant disciplines and ideologies which involves the task of developing propositions about the increasignly complex international relationships. Thus peace research has to be, as Galtung holds, cross-disciplinary, cross-ideological, theoretically oriented, and concerned with applicability.[3]

[1] Institute for Social Research, *Research for Peace Essays* (Amsterdam, 1954).
[2] Johan Galtung, "A Critical Definition of Peace Research", *Our Generation Against Nuclear War* (Montreal), Vol. 3, October 1964, pp. 4-21.
[3] Johan Galtung has also prepared a paper, viz., "Peace Research" in which he has examined various trends and orientations in peace research and

There are two other articles which have to be noted on the meaning of peace research. One is "Peace Research: Outline of an Inquiry into Causes, Effects, and Problems"[4] by Leo Hamon and the other is "National and International Peace Research"[5] by Bert Roling. While Hamon argues that peace research should concentrate on deducting the shape of a possible warless world from trends already discernible rather than on the basis of utopiansim, Roling emphasizes that peace research must deal not only with intentional war but also with unintentional war. There is no apparent controversy between the points of emphasis made by Hamon and Roling in their respective papers. Both of them have analysed the problem of defining the purpose and scope of peace research from a different angle. But the object is the same: defining peace research. Hamon holds that the declining position of power bipolarity is fast creating self-stabilizing effects of continuing peace. He opines that internal developments within countries, population growth, technical progress, and inequalities in living standards tend to replace violence as the chief coordinators of the game of power. Roling asserts that peace researchers have to concern themselves with four problems: the phenomenonlogy of war, what is necessary for survival, what is possible in the world, and whether we can make possible that which is necessary. Thus both Hamon and Roling insist on that which is possible. As such, a definition of peace research deducible from their papers would be that peace research is a pursuit after analysing factors leading to conflict situations and those contributig to the maintenance of the current state of warlessness. There is yet

---

its relationships with other disciplines. The paper is available in mimeographed form from the Peace Research Institute, Oslo. There is another paper published by Galtung under the title *After the First Years—What? Some Notes on the Long Term Development of Peace Research* (Peace Research Institute, Oslo, 1964). This publication is in the nature of stock-taking of peace research. Galtung is also reported to have defined peace research in his introduction to *International Reportory of Disarmament and Peace Research Institutions*, to be published soon jointly by the Unesco and Peace Research Institute, Oslo.

[4] Leo Hamon, "Peace Research:Outline of an Inquiry into Causes, Effects, and Problems", *International Social Science Journal: Peace Research* (Paris), Vol. 17, No. 3, 1965, pp. 420-41.

[5] Bert V.A. Roling, "National and International Peace Research", *International Social Science Journal: Peace Research*, Vol. 17, No. 3, 1965, pp. 487-505.

another interesting article dealing with the meaning of peace research. This is "Meaning and Purpose of Peace Research"[6] by Norman Alcock. According to Alcock, peace research is the answer to a felt need for the elimination of war.

In fact, peace research has still a long way to becoming a discipline. Therefore, it is not surprising that a broadly acceptable definition of peace research has not yet been formulated. But scholars working in the field have certainly left hints about the possible dimensions of peace research. John Burton, for example, holds in his "Peace Research and International Relations"[7] that the recent breakthrough in the field of international politics and the greater concern for peace research will make the distinction between international politics and peace research disappear. His argument appears to be something like this: The concern for peace puts a serious check upon national units in their freedom of behaviour in international relationships. Therefore, the concept of international politics as a pattern of unrestricted struggle for power must change in the light of the importance we have come to attach to peace. This approach also seems to dominate Burton's another work, namely *Peace Theory: Preconditions of Disarmament*.[8] In both his article and in his book Burton points out the growing possibility of the emergence of a new discipline of peace research and deals with the problem of how social change can be dealt with creatively. Theo Lentz goes even a step further and asserts in his *Towards a science of Peace*[9] that we are fast moving in the direction of having a science of peace. Lentz holds that our world needs nothing so immediately as the elimination of war and that for this we lack necessary and adequate understanding. Therefore, he suggests that serious and organized search for this knowledge ought to be our greatest imperative. Lentz points out the characteristics of this knowledge in detail. He stresses the need for wider dissemination of knowledge and for fuller discussion of scientific

[6] Norman Z. Alcock, "The Meaning and Purpose of Peace Research", *Gandhi Marg* (New Delhi), Vol. 9, July 1865, pp. 204-14.
[7] John W. Burton, "Peace Research and International Relations", *Journal of Conflict Resolution* (Chicago), Vol. 8, September 1964, pp. 281-86.
[8] John W. Burton, *Peace Theory: Preconditions of Disarmament* (New York, 1962).
[9] Theo F. Lentz, *Towards A Science of Peace* (New York, 1961), 2nd edition.

facts and ideas at all levels of society.

There are some articles containing suggestions about possibilities of research on peace. They have been issued by various research centres and are very useful for constructing a definition of peace research. Chief among such articles are "Peace Research Priorities"[10], "Outline and Classification of the Problems of Peace Research"[11], and *Documentation in the Social Sciences*.[12] In all of them, an effort has been made to point out possible subjects of research which may contribute to the basic purpose of peace research and thus they reveal various unstated shades of the meaning of peace research. Equally important should be the forthcoming publications by L. Leonard and Karl Birnbaum, namely *Development and Significance of Peace Research*[13] and *Memorandum on Peace Research*[14]. The latter, however, has been written in the Swedish language. But its English translation is expected to be available soon. On the basis of what has been reported about it so far, it can be indicated here that it examines the state of the field of peace research and various concepts of what peace research should be. Birnbaum divides peace research into two main approaches: research on the conditions of peace and the nature of conflict; and research on security policy and strategy including arms control. Mention can also be made here of "Research Into Problems of War and Peace"[15] by Edgar Anstey.

What about the quality of work that has been done so far in the field of peace research? A number of endeavours, at both the individual and organizational levels, are in process and one must know what those endeavours have achieved either in analysing the nature of the problem of peace or in crystallizing the attitude of people towards peace. An admirable account of the achievements of peace research has been given

---

[10] Peace Research Institute of Washington, "Peace Research Priorities", mimeographed.
[11] "Outline and Classification of the Problems of Peace Research", *Peace Research: News and Views* (New York), September 1964, pp. 27-38.
[12] Unesco, *Documentation in the Social Sciences* (Paris, 1963).
[13] L. Leonard, *Development and Significance of Peace Research*, to be published.
[14] Karl E. Birnbaum, *Memorandum on Peace Research*, to be published.
[15] Edgar Anstey, "Research Into Problems of War and Peace", *Occupational Psychology* (London), Vol. 43, pp. 193-207.

by Martin Oppenheimer and Arthur Waskow in their respective articles "Peace Research Game"[16] and "Peace Research Reality".[17] Openheimer believes that peace research has considerably undermined the view that arms race emanates from inherent socio-economic and political nature of the capitalist and socialist societies. Even if one does not agree with this view, one has to admit that no single factor can be held to be absolutely responsible for the threat to peace. This view of Oppenheimer also brings home the truth that the problem of peace requires a clear grasp of the underlying dynamics of social systems as also of the problem of how to change them. Waskow's article is in many ways a critique of Oppenheimer's. Waskow's main criticism is that model-building and small group research for peace are not, as Openheimer thinks, unnecessary. Both of them, in his view, generate some valuable hypotheses on the control of conflict and the containment of violence. Peace research should be theoretical, it should be experimental, and it should also be historical. This is a sane view indeed. For the results of such a multi-dimensional research may make it politically, and also perhaps intellectually, possible to create new world policies favourable to the cause of peace.

PEACE RESEARCH AND NONVIOLENCE

Peace research and nonviolence are closely interconnected. For the former is the means to the realization of the values laid down by the latter. But there has been a great deal of discussion even with regard to the meaning of nonviolence and the content of values it propounds. However, we have had more definitive works on the meaning of nonviolence than on the meaning of peace research. Therefore, it would be appropriate to include in this survey select items on the meaning of nonviolence. In spite of growing awareness of the importance of nonviolence, there is widespread confusion about what nonviolence is or means. Unless a precise definition of

[16] Martin Oppenheimer, "Peace Research Game", *Dissent* (New York), Vol. 11, Autumn 1964, pp. 444-47.
[17] Arthur I. Waskow, "Peace Research Reality", *Dissent,* Vol. 11, Autumn 1964, pp. 448-50.

the term is evolved, a study of the relevance of nonviolence in international relations may not prove fruitful. In other words, a serious attempt should be made to examine the feasibility of reconstructing a theory of nonviolence applicable to international relations. The material surveyed in this section covers various shades of meaning attached to the term "nonviolence". As the purpose here is to bring to light the fundamental postulates of nonviolence, as enunciated by different scholars, which may help building up such a theory, only such publications are reviewed here as are significant and relevant.

The study of nonviolence from what may be called a sociological angle was never more important than today. Although nonviolence is generally taken to mean absence of physical violence against human beings, clarity of thought about it has often been handicapped by both proponents and opponents of nonviolence. It is here that the sociological approach is most helpful. Emphasis on the importance of this approach for the study of nonviolence has been a comparatively recent development. There are, however, a few studies published fairly long ago which give a deep insight into the sociological interpretation of nonviolence and which are relevant even to peace research today. One such study is *Nonviolent Coercion: A Study in Methods of Social Pressure*[18] by Clarence Marsh Case. The title of the book looks somewhat incongruous; yet this extraordinary combination— "nonviolence" and "coercion" is not unnatural. Coercion means compelling another party to take a particular course of action against his will. If, therefore, the term is reinterpreted to mean compelling the evil-doer not to do evil, it is a happy expression and it becomes still more important if this type of coercion is possible with nonviolent means. How nonviolent coercion is possible is precisely the problem of Case's book. The plan of the book is, first, to trace the origins and earlier history of the idea of nonviolence and of the quaintly picturesque sects like the Bohemian Brethren, the Anabaptists, the Mennonites, the Doukhobors, and the Quakers etc., which have given to nonviolence an organized

[18] Clarence Marsh Case, *Nonviolent Coercion: A Study in Methods of Social Pressure* (London, 1923).

expression. Then follow certain interpretative chapters seeking to explain the logical difficulties, psychological bases, and practical effectiveness or futility of nonviolence. In the final few chapters the author distinguishes between the older form of nonviolent movement and its later phase as expressed in the strike, the boycott, and non-co-operation. He also examines the bearing of nonviolence on problems of democracy and social idealism. Not only is the treatment of the subject couched in the terminology of sociology but the whole problem is examined from the point of view of the relevance of nonviolence in various kinds of social groups. Some of the specific questions discussed by Case are: What have been the social antecedents and the significance of the individuals and groups that have stood for the principle of nonviolence? What innate and acquired traits underlie it? What social attitudes, heritages, conditions, and value-systems promote it? What specific technique is required to modify nonviolently the behaviour of social groups such as sects, neighbourhoods, or nations? How far has the practice and preaching of nonviolence influenced the ideas, feelings, and actions of men and groups and how far has it made an impress upon public opinion, political and social institutions, and governmental policy? What value does nonviolence have for the resistance of aggression and for the accomplishment of desired social goals?

Case has dealt with these questions in the context of three basic problems: individual resistance, intra-group resistance, and inter-group resistance which also includes international wars. Thus Case has developed in his book a sociological concept of nonviolence. Although the book was written in the background of the conditions created by the First World War, it has great value even today to those engaged in peace research, because the problems discussed in it are more relevant now than ever before. Case has brought out subtle distinctions between various terms connected with nonviolence—terms like passive resistance, non-resistance, nonviolent resistance, pacifism, and conscientious objection. But so much has been said on, and done with, nonviolence since the publication of Case's book that many of its conclusions have to be re-examined in order to understand how and what type of nonviolence can be applied to international relations now. But doing that is precisely the function of peace research.

It has often been found that those who reject violence on grounds of principle have rarely analysed the relation of their belief systems with those of others who are also opposed to violence. But some of them have recognized differences in motivation and behaviour among those rejecting violence. For example, Guy Hershberger, in his article, "Biblical Non-Resistance and Modern Pacifism"[19], distinguishes between "non-resistance" and "modern pacifism". The former, according to him, reflects the faith and life of those who cannot take any part in warfare and who renounce all coercion, even nonviolent; the latter is a term which covers many types of opposition to war. But the treatment of this article is just superficial, for it does not examine pacifism from a sociological angle. This is what Johan Galtung has done in his "Pacifism From a Sociological Point of View."[20] The merit of this paper lies in the fact that it not only defines pacifism with the help of sociological theories and concepts, but it also clarifies some theoretical problems of what may be called the sociology of pacifism and also points out some hypotheses which might not only be validated theoretically but may also be tested empirically. Reginald Reynolds' "What Are Pacifists Doing?"[21] enunciates a distinction between western pacifism and Gandhian pacifism and comes to the conclusion that wheareas the former only seeks to avoid war mainly by refusing to fight and by carrying on propaganda against war, the latter goes much deeper and aims at the eradication of the seeds of war from the social and economic life of man. A recent publication, *Pacifism: An Historical and Sociological Study*[22], by David Martin can also be mentioned here. It gives a general discussion of the roots of pacifism[23].

---

[19] Guy F. Hershberger, "Biblical Non-Resistance and Modern Pacificism", *Mennonite Quarterly Review* (Goshen), Vol. 17, July 1943, pp. 87-99.

[20] Johan Galtung, "Pacifism From a Sociological Point of View", *Journal of Conflict Resolution,* Vol. 3, March 1959, pp. 67-84.

[21] Reginald Reynolds, "What Are Pacifists Doing?", *Peace News* (London), 20 July 1956.

[22] David A. Martin, *Pacifism: An Historical and Sociological Study* (London, 1965).

[23] It is reported that Giuliano Pontara has recently completed a study on Gandhi and western pacifism and that it would be soon made available.

Political Theories of Modern Pacifism : An Analysis and Criticism[24] by Mulford Sibley is another work of some value. The author distinguishes between three types of nonviolence: Hindu pacifism (Satyagraha), Christian pacifism, and revolutionary secular pacifism. But this classification is rather narrow in scope inasmuch as it only covers modern types of pacifism and ignores nonviolence as such. It cannot, therefore, be recommended as a full typology of nonviolence. There is another work which, though important otherwise, suffers from the same defect. This is *Passive Resistance in South Africa*[25] by L. Kuper. But on the whole both these works provide helpful material for the reconstruction of a viable theory of nonviolence.

One writer who can claim to have developed, though unintentionally, some form of a typology of nonviolence is Theodore Paullin. In his *Introduction to Non-Violence*[26], intended to be an attempt at considering the application of nonviolent means in achieving group purposes, he describes six types of nonviolence. His classification, though not definitive, is indeed a contribution towards developing a scientific interpretation of nonviolence. A more elaborate treatment has been presented by Gene Sharp in his article "Meanings of Nonviolence".[27] His classification assumes various forms of nonviolence some of which tally with those described by Paullin. The first of these forms is "generic nonviolence" by which Sharp means the whole system of belief and behaviour characterized by abstention from physical violence. Thus it is a very wide term including almost all varieties of nonviolence. It may be said in all fairness that all the types of nonviolence mentioned by Sharp are only various types of generic nonviolence. Next comes "pacifism" which Sharp defines as a belief-system of those who, as a minimum, refuse participation in all wars on moral, ethical, or religious principles. The third type is "nonviolent resistance and direct action" which refers to those

[24] Mulford Q. Sibley, *Political Theories of Modern Pacifism: An Analysis and Criticism* (Philadelphia, 1944).
[25] L. Kuper, *Passive Resistance in South Africa* (London, 1956).
[26] Theodore Paullin, *Introduction to Non-violence* (Philadelphia, 1944).
[27] Gene Sharp, "The Meanings of Non-violence", *Journal of Conflict Resolution*, Vol. 3, March 1959, pp. 41-64.

methods without physical violence that may be called extra-constitutional. The fourth form is "non-resistance" the advocates of which reject, on principle, all physical force, whether at individual, State, or international level. "Active reconciliation" refers, according to Sharp, to that category of nonviolence which favours the use of active goodwill and reconciliation as a principle. Then there is "moral resistance" —again a matter of principle—which maintains that all evil should be positively resisted but only by peaceful and moral means. The concept of "selective nonviolence" means refusal to participate in major violent conflicts, particularly international wars. "Passive resistance" is, to Sharp, a method of conducting conflicts and achieving one type of social, economic and political set-up and thwarting another. But it is preferred only to physical violence and is not based on any principle. In contrast to passive resistance, "peaceful resistance" has a relatively widespread recognition in nonviolent methods as being intrinsically better than violence. "Satyagrah", according to Sharp, is a type of generic nonviolence developed by Gandhi who meant by it an effort at attainment of Truth through love and right actions and for whom it is a matter of principle. The last form of nonviolence in Sharp's classification is "nonviolent revolution", the votaries of which believe that the root cause of all our ills lies in individual and social life and, therefore, they can be remedied only by a revolutionary change in individuals and society. One may or may not agree with Sharp's classification but it certainly helps in clarifying the existing confusion about various approaches to nonviolence. William Robert Miller has also attempted a classification of various shades of nonviolence in his book *Nonviolence: A Christian Interpretation*[28]. He devotes one section to the various meanings and shades of nonviolence and another to the actual conduct of nonviolent action. Within the context of these two sections he also discusses the problem of nonviolent national defence and that of an international nonviolent peace force. Besides, he discusses some examples of the use of nonviolence in various parts of the world.

[28] William Robert Miller, *Nonviolence: A Christian Interpretation* (London, 1964).

There are two articles which have been recently published and which are very useful in the context of the meaning of nonviolence. They are "What Does Nonviolence Mean?"[29] by LeRoi Jones and "On the Meaning of Nonviolence"[30] by Johan Galtung. While the former examines the meaning of nonviolence in a particular context of the Negro resistance against the Whites, the latter studies nonviolence in a purely general framework. The questions to which LeRoi Jones addresses himself are: What is the nature and character of the Negro resistance? What prospects does it offer of enlarging the area of the application of nonviolence? How far is that resistance really nonviolent? He examines and analyses one among several points of view that are gaining currency among Negores amidst the mounting racial crisis in the United States. The author holds that violence or nonviolence have not been real categories and that their use is only symbolic. According to him, they mean different things to different people. For example, a White man understands by violence a threat to his system or a possibility of outright war to change the political and economic patterns. LeRoi Jones' contention is that the bourgeois black man in America does not want a complete withdrawal from White society, which is possible only by a political rebellion. And a political rebellion is taken both by the bourgeois black and the White man to constitute violence. The nature of the black man's oppression also makes any organized violence almost impossible. Therefore, the result is that nonviolence as a theory of social and political group behaviour among the American Negroes is simply a continuance of the status quo. This theory is utilized by the White man to contend that the black man must participate as a privileged class among the oppressed. This is what the author of the article regards as the "most sinister application of the Western method of confusing and subjugating peoples". The conclusion he draws is that nonviolence and passive resistance are only the "echoes of a contemporary redefinition of the Negro's place". He also holds that the

---

[29] LeRoi Jones, "What Does Nonviolence Mean?", *Midstream* (New York), Vol. 9, December 1963, pp. 33-44.
[30] Johan Galtung, "On the Meaning of Nonviolence", *Journal of Peace Research* (Oslo), 1965, pp. 228-57.

general psychology of an average Negro is that, irrespective of whatever is going on in the form of a war against racial discrimination, no substantial help is being offered to him at all. In this connexion he examines several cases of the grant of civil rights to Negroes and makes a number of bold statements including the one that the desegregation of schools has been largely illusory.

The basic point LeRoi Jones makes is that in the context of Negro resistance, nonviolence means no action at all, and, therefore, it is not likely to be a helpful moral concept in the social environment of America, specially in South America. The point is no doubt important. But the answer to the question, "What does nonviolence mean?" is rather round-about, inasmuch as it only tells us how and why there is no nonviolence in the case of Negro resistance, without developing a scientific typology of nonviolence and then using it as a criterion for determining the violent or nonviolent character of that resistance. Nonviolence, after all, is not a cloistered virtue but a principle to be applied in intergroup and intragroup relations. But this application requires a continuous experimentation with its strategy and technique. A scholar's task is to make an objective study of such experiments wherever and whenever they are made with a view to finding out which nonviolent methods can be successful in which type of circumstances. Such an objective study proceeds with the assumption that any experiment of this nature is likely to enrich the potentialities of nonviolence as a technique. As such, the evolution of an effective technique of nonviolence has to be, besides other things, a matter of reconstruction. Unfortunately this is what LeRoi Jones's analysis tends to ignore. The title of his article suggests that one can expect the author to point out some new dimensions of nonviolence as reflected in the Negro resistance which would be useful for the reconstruction of an effective technique of nonviolence. But his approach is essentially a negative one and it leads him to believe that nonviolence in the southern United States is not being used as a means but has become an end for the Whites and middle class Negroes, that the Negroes have no goal to work towards, and that they have no programme of political rebellion against the status quo. But the seriousness of LeRoi Jones' article consists not only in his thesis that there is no discernible use of violence in the Negroes' fight against racialism but also in his suggestion that only schemes of socio-economic reconstruction, and not nonviolence, can improve the lot of the Negroes. In fact, emphasis on nonviolence, in his opinion, would only speed the coming of a serious crisis. One may not agree with this negative approach and pessimism. But the article is an interesting sociological study of the subject, because it presents a new point of view and also because it opens up an avenue for further research, that is, for a study of the subject with a positive approach.

Galtung studies nonviolence in his own definitional framework without depending on whatever the proponents of nonviolence may have said about it. Galtung defines nonviolence as an effort to influence, and then builds a typology of influence techniques. He identifies nonviolence both in its negative and positive aspects, the former referring to techniques that impede the execution of negative actions and the latter to techniques that facilitate the execution of positive actions. It is Galtung's belief that the future of nonviolence depends on the development of positive techniques. By virtue of being of a theoretical nature, Galtung's article is of greater utility than LeRoi Jones'.

GANDHI AND POSSIBILITIES OF RESEARCH ON PEACE

Actually nonviolence is the value around which peace research should revolve. Nonviolence has been preached and practised in all the known periods of human history. But it is Gandhi to whom belongs the credit of bringing nonviolence to its latest phase. Therefore, anyone who is interested in a correct understanding of nonviolence cannot ignore the Gandhian contribution. As the need for finding out alternatives to force and violence is growing, the efforts to discover Gandhi's relevance are also being intensified. Some of these efforts ought to be classified as a part of peace research. For even in examing the relevance of Gandhi today their focus is on discovering those aspects of Gandhian thinking which, by reinterpretation, can be helpful in the creation of peaceful human relations. It would be advisable, therefore, to include in this survey a few important publications on Gandhi. Two such important publications are *Gandhi On World Affairs*[31] and "Toward A Re-evaluation of Gandhi's Political Thought,"[32] both by Paul Power. The first publication is an attempt at discerning the principles of nonviolence applicable to international affairs. The purpose of the author is to bring together Gandhi's main ideas on world affairs and to evaluate their present relevance. While in the former purpose the author seems to have succeeded partly, in the latter he falls short of expectations. Further, the two chapters containing Gandhi's biography and his political philosophy do not belong to a book like Power's dealing with the impact of Gandhian nonviolence on world affairs. In his article, however, Power's concern is to examine whether the ingredients of Gandhi's thought constitute a political philosophy and in performing this task he discusses two such aspects of Gandhian thinking as are important for peace research. These two aspects are: the nature and limits of political obligation and the ethical premises of peaceful change. Likewise, W.H. Morris-Jones' article on "Mahatma Gandhi—Political Philosopher?"[33], though primarily concerned with Gandhi's political philosophy, is also indirectly useful for peace researchers.

For quite a long time there has been a need for a comprehensive study examining the relevance of Gandhian techniques today. The publication of *Gandhi: His Relevance for Our Times*,[34] edited by G. Ramachandran and T.K. Mahadevan, fulfils this need to some extent. Presented to Sri R.R. Diwakar on his seventieth birthday, this volume includes essays on various aspects of Gandhian philosophy whose relevance in the contemporary world requires a careful analysis. This is not to say that all the essays discuss the question of Gandhi's relevance today. Some of them are, of course,

[31] Paul F. Power, *Gandhi on World Affairs* (Washington, D.C., 1960).
[32] Paul F. Power, "Toward A Re-evaluation of Gandhi's Political Thought", *Western Political Quarterly* (Salt Lake City), Vol. 16, March 1963, pp. 99-108.
[33] W.H. Morris-Jones, "Mahatma Gandhi—Political Philosopher?", *Political Studies* (London), Vol. 8, February 1960, pp. 16-36.
[34] G. Ramachandran and T.K. Mahadevan, eds., *Gandhi: His Relevance for Our Times* (Bombay, 1964).

concerned merely with a statement of the spiritual or moral bases of Gandhi's thinking and some of them are primarily of only casual interest. But some of them deal with the basic question as to whether and how the Gandhian technique can be successful in resolving conflicts and thus in ensuring peace. Among such essays may be counted "Gandhi's Political Significance Today" by Gene Sharp, "Violence and Power Politics" by Stephen King-Hall, "Experimentation in Nonviolence: the Next Phase" by William Robert Miller, "A Nonviolent International Authority" by Ted Dunn, and "A Gandhian Model for World Politics" by Paul Power.

The main focus in Gene Sharp's attempt to examine Gandhi's relevance today is on dispelling the commonplace notions that lead to a belief in the unsuitability of Gandhi to our problems of today. Sharp believes that Gandhi's philosophy and technique are important for the world as a whole and not for India alone. The conclusion to which he is led is that the most significant contribution of Gandhi was in creating an awareness in people that war could be avoided as a means to the resolution of conflicts. This awareness itself demands a search for an alternative to war. And Sharp is right in holding that this search is much more needed today than ever before. However, Sharp does not take up the question of how this search should be carried on or what can be the alternative to war. The question is difficult indeed. But Stephen King-Hall suggests a way which would perhaps be helpful in our search for such an alternative. The way is to change the nature of the relationship between violence and international politics and this can be done, in King-Hall's opinion, by putting the use of nuclear power under the control of an international organization.

William Robert Miller is concerned in his essay with the lessons that can be drawn from the experiments in the use of nonviolence and which could be our guide today. Although he takes up two such experiments, one from India and the other from the United States, the sweep of his generalizations is remarkable. And he writes with conviction that violence has got to be done away with from human society. He has, of course, not answered the question as to how it can be done.

This is a most difficult question. But he has at least succeeded in conveying that man has lost faith in violence and that something should be done to find out an alternative to violence and in appealing to us to take steps to make the next phase of nonviolence more successful.

Ted Dunn takes up the problem of the use of nonviolence today at a deeper level. He strikes a note of understanding of the present human situation when he says that the problems of today are not the same that Gandhi faced inasmuch as Gandhi's objective was to regain freedom, whereas the main challenge to the nations today is how to preserve freedom. This fact should always be borne in mind in all our efforts for evolving a successful nonviolent technique that could be applicable today. This further strengthens the view that a Gandhian or nonviolent technique which could be relevant today is essentially a matter of reconstruction.

Paul Power builds a Gandhian model of world politics. Behind it is his assumption that the Gandhian technique of nonviolence can be successful today only if a definite type of international society is evolved. And this can be possible if the values cherished by Gandhi are expanded far enough to be characteristic of international politics. The logic of such an assumption would persuade us to believe that the Gandhian technique can be relevant only in a particular type of setting. Power may or may not agree with it. But it certainly rasises an interesting problem requiring careful investigation.

Taken as a whole, the contributions to the volume *Gandhi: His Relevance for Our Times* point to a faith in Gandhi's relevance today and a hope in Gandhi's success in future. As a matter of fact, this faith and this hope constitute an important basis for the furtherance of peace research. Those from the west who have contributed to this volume have even otherwise been doing commendable work in the field of peace research and their work sometimes appears to throw the challenge that real, scientific work on Gandhi can be done only in the west. The book presently under survey can be taken as a beginning of the desire to accept the challenge. But let us not stop at accepting it. We must proceed further to meet it.

Gandhi and the Nuclear Age[35] by Arne Naess is also concerned with an examination of Gandhi's current relevance. Naess is not satisfied with the purely moral argument for nonviolence. He indicates how Gandhian principles may provide a practical approach to modern international conflicts. He presents a five-point programme for a peaceful state, including an outline of a "non-coercive foreign policy" and a "non-military defence policy". The suggestions made by Naess are worth examing in the context of each nation. Mention may also be made here of a special issue of the journal *Seminar*[36] devoted to an assessment of the current relevance of Gandhi's theory of truth and nonviolence.

One who is interested in the relevance of nonviolence to the present problem of peace cannot afford to ignore a recent, edited publication entitled *The Emerging World*[37]. Brought out as a Jawaharlal Nehru Memorial Volume, it covers a variety of subjects like peaceful change and scientific progress, economic development and the enlargement of higher values, and a better future for mankind. But the essays that deserve special attention in a survey like this are two. They are: "World Morality and World Peace" by Linus Pauling and "Towards One World by Peaceful Change" by Arnold Toynbee. Pauling thinks that the problem of world peace is a problem of world morality. That is more or less theme of Toynbee's paper also, though Toynbee's emphasis is on what he calls the spiritual unification of the world.

Joan Bondurant's *Conquest of Violence*[38] is the first attempt at abstracting from Gandhi's experiments with *Satyagrah* a theoretical key to the problems of social and political conflict. The author maintains that nonviolence as an ethical principle is a technique of social action and that, as such, it does not depend upon Gandhi's teaching in matters like vegetarianism, sexual continence, or non-possession. She also asserts that nonviolence is not simply a manifestation of Hindu tradition. She has also argued persuasively that the success of the

---

[35] Arne Naess, *Gandhi and the Nuclear Age* (Totowa, New Jersey, 1965).
[36] "Gandhism: A Symposium on the Theory and Practice of Nonviolence and Truth", *Seminar* (New Delhi), No. 46, June 1963.
[37] Jawaharlal Nehru Souvenir Volume Committee, *The Emerging World* (Bombay, 14 November 1964).
[38] Joan V. Bondurant, *Conquest of Violence* (Princeton, 1958).

Gandhian method is not dependent upon Gandhi's metaphysical assumptions nor upon his Hindu-based theology. Traditional Indian thought and modern western thought have both, she holds, influenced the theory and philosophy of *Satyagrah*. Therefore, according to her, the Hindu milieu is not necessary for acceptance, application, and success of nonviolence as a technique. It could operate successfully in even non-Hindu societies as it actually did among the Muslim Pathans of the North-West Frontier Province (the Khudai Khidmatgar movement).

Perhaps the best part of Bondurant's book is the last chapter, namely "Gandhian Dialectic and Political Theory". The author presents therein a theoretical framework for the Gandhian philosophy of conflict and examines its relevance to contemporary political theory and problems. She considers the Gandhian emphasis on the moral approximation of end and means as a sort of a "dialectic" which views means as "ends-in-the-making". She views the Gandhian dialectic, in contrast to the Hegelian and Marxian dialectic, not as descriptive of society but as a process to be applied in resolving conflicts and producing an entirely new circumstance. Bondurant brings out the essential weakness of the absence of power recognition of the end-means relationship in anarchism, conservatism, authoritarian idealism, and even liberalism, and then shows how the Gandhian technique is relevant to meeting this weakness. Her book is indeed of outstanding value in that it demonstrates that there is a large area for theoretical analysis of nonviolence in the light of nonviolent methods of socio-political action. It is an illustration from a particular discipline of the richness of the new field and no one who is interested in peace research can afford to miss Bondurant's volume. However, her lack of clarity in the use of terms is a little regrettable. For example, although Bondurant correctly contrasts the term "non-resistance" with "Satyagrah", she ignores several existing uses of the term by which various schools of pacifist thought are described. Nevertheless, the book offers rich material for a rational reconstruction of nonviolent technique in the form of a normative system.

"A Systematization of Gandhian Ethics of Conflict

Resolution"[39] by Arne Naess offers excellent exposition of those nonviolent attitudes that have crystallized into more or less explicit ethical doctrines. By "the ethics of nonviolence" Naess means a normative and systematic ethics containing a general norm against violence (excluding war for defensive purposes). This general norm, according to him, is that we should act in a group struggle in a way conducive to long-term universal reduction of violence. In his article, Naess has presented us with an analysis of such an ethics of nonviolence in a condensed, systematized form. The primary sources on which he has depended for this kind of inquiry are historical documents and the material pertaining to Gandhi's activities, his writings, and his correspondence, speeches and conversations. The systematization of Gandhian ethics of conflict resolution done by Naess is the first undertaking of its kind. Although it covers Gandhi's ethics of group struggle relating to the period 1907-34 only, yet it can provide a useful basis for the reconstruction of a more adequate theory of nonviolence which could be applicable in the resolution of intergroup conflicts.

Very recently a few other articles of considerable merit were also published on Gandhism. Each of them, though following different approaches, attempts to reinterpret Gandhi's ideas and reassess their relevance critically in the context of modern circumstances and problems.

One of them is "Gandhism Re-Examined"[40] by Ashakant Nimbark. In it, the author starts with the assumption that it is very difficult today to measure the role of outstanding individuals in social and cultural change and to determine the place of ideologies and ethics in politics. Nevertheless, he attempts an examination of the scope, value, and current relevance of the work and thought of Gandhi, whom he describes, and rightly so, as a charismatic leader. Nimbark essays to perform his task by addressing himself to five questions: the development of Gandhian ideology as a whole, the present position of Gandhism in Indian politics, Gandhian

---

[39] Arne Naess, "A Systematization of Gandhian Ethics of Conflict Resolution", *Journal of Conflict Resolution,* Vol. 2, June 1958, pp. 140-55.
[40] Ashakant Nimbark, "Gandhism Re-Examined", *Social Research* (New York), Vol. 31, March 1964, pp. 94-125.

economic theory, the current relevance of Gandhism to human relations in general, and the applicability of Gandhian techniques to race relations in particular.

Analysing Gandhism in retrospect, Nimbark holds that the main tenets of Gandhi's political philosophy were non-violence, decentralization of power, and freedom for all, although in the process of his own political maturation Gandhi did make occasional compromises and revisions. Gandhian phiolosophy, asserts Nimbark, allows and even encourages dissent and, unlike Marxism, adopts an anti-deterministic approach. It is the contention of the author, however, that after the attainment of independence Indians have preserved and glorified Gandhi's ideals only in spirit and on occasions have even used Gandhi's own elastic tenets to justify what Nimbark calls their non-Gandhian behaviour. In other countries also Gandhian principles have been followed only selectively. The main point that Nimbark makes in the first section of his article is that Gandhian philosophy has become a sort of an ideological bible from which different people can find support for their current needs. On the other hand, there are people who realize that the "experiments with truth" did not end with Gandhi's death and that they should be carried further.

This leads the author to an examination of Gandhism in current Indian politics. The issue which he discusses in the main is the dilemma between India's faith in peace and non-violence and her defence expenditure. Nimbark holds that even Gandhi's political ideas were caught in the dilemma between what Max Weber called "ethic of ultimate ends" and "ethic of responsibility". And this dilemma is still more serious for the statesmen of India. This dilemma is sometimes viewed negatively as national schism and ideological inconsistency but, if viewed positively, it can also provide a basis for developing a new, realistic, pragmatic approach to power politics. As a matter of fact, contemporary Indian Gandhians are attacked both by extreme pacifists like Bertrand Russell and by extreme realists. Therefore, the dilemma of an absolute end versus responsibility has not yet been resolved. Nimbark is right in pointing out that on the problem of war Gandhi as an ideologist would advocate "peace at any price", while as a responsible nationalist leader he would accept "peace, but not at any price". Thus the dilemma mentioned above is not an indication of a logical inconsistency but a pointer to the need for carrying the Gandhian experiment further and exploring and elaborating new methods of Satyagrah which can be used both in the guaranteeing of social justice and protection of national rights and in the maintenance of peace. This is not to say that Gandhism is an incomplete philosophy but that an experiment in the application of the Gandhian technique to international relations has yet to be made.

In a generic sense, the problem of peace research is connected with the problem of resolution of human conflicts. Gandhi did, of course, advocate "supreme consideration" to man as an individual. But he was also aware of the Hobbesian problem of order. The Gandhian solution to the problem of individual freedom versus social obstacles is a middle way between the two extremes—group-centred and power-led human actions on the one hand and unguided or normless conduct on the other. The Gandhian technique of resolving human conflicts is directly concerned with the question as to how this balance should be maintained. Nimbark examines this theory in the light of the sociological research done by scholars like Karl Jaspers, Hannah Arendt, Erich Fromm, Vincent Sheean, Joan Bondurant, Gene Sharp, and Arne Naess. An attempt has been made by him to trace briefly the similarities and dissimilarities between Gandhi and some scholars in regard to both their theoretical postulates and their techniques. Together with this he also tries to assess the nature of Gandhi's impact on modern peaceful methods of conflict resolution and in so doing he answers some of the criticisms levelled against the Gandhian theory of conflict resolution. For example, he does not endorse the criticism that self-suffering and non-attachment—two important aspects of Gandhian Satyagraha—run counter to the ideals of freedom and nonviolence. As the criticism goes, self-suffering is self-violence and non-attachment is a contradiction in terms because a free man is to look for more alternatives and better opportunities rather than to detach himself from the world of choices. It is the conviction of Nimbark that "in an effort to maintain self-respect and dignity, modern man sometimes has no better tool than self-sacrifice". Nimbark also holds that the west could emulate Gandhian philosophy in relevant situations, that the inadequacy of Gandhi's influence in Indian politics should not obscure the long-range universal relevance of Gandhi's methods, and that these methods can be successful in the resolution of human conflicts in any society. Nimbark cites many cases in which Gandhian methods have been used outside India. He contends that the question about the practical relevance and continuing influence of Gandhi today can be tackled in either of the two ways: by examining the historical and theoretical aspects of Gandhism or by taking into account the surviving influence of Gandhi in specific areas. The former way is the way of confusion leading to the possible conclusion that Gandhism is no longer relevant. Therefore, Nimbark's advice is to follow the latter way in which case Gandhism must be evaluated in terms of its applicability not only in India but elsewhere too, for the importance of Gandhi's ideas cannot be allowed to remain confined to India as the importance of J.S. Mill's ideas has not been confined to Britain.

Thus Nimbark writes with sympathy and with hope about Gandhism and about its current relevance. Unlike him, the approach adopted by Hugh Tinker in his article, "Magnificent Failure: The Gandhian Ideal in India After Sixteen Years"[41], is one of downright and deliberate criticism. Tinker's contention is that in India only the Gandhian spirit of dedication survives. His study is primarily based upon a close study of Gandhi's life and ideals and then on an analysis of how the social, economic and political programme of independent India indicates a departure from what Gandhi had preached and practised. He is confronted with two interpretations of Gandhi: as a religious phenomenon and as a symbol of fight against imperialism. And his conclusion is that the essence of Gandhi's political creed was compromise, conciliation, and cooperation, and that the extent of success or failure of Gandhi in independent India can be judged by the extent to which this creed has or has not been furthered. Various illustrations have been given in Tinker's article to

[41] Hugh Tinker, "Magnificent Failure: The Gandhian Ideal in India After Sixteen Years", *International Affairs* (London), Vol. 40, April 1964, pp. 262-76.

show that Gandhi believed in a political method, the chief ingredients of which were compromise, conciliation, and cooperation. Conciliation, in Tinker's opinion, was the culmination of Gandhi's effort to introduce morality into politics. His reason for such a contention is that dealing with his Congress colleagues who had love for power, which Gandhi resented very much and which he also considered to be a decline from absolute standards, he could only try for cooperation, compromise, and conciliation. All this, no doubt, shows Tinker's profound understanding of Gandhi's methods. But this very understanding brings him into a serious realm of contradictions *vis-a-vis* a few of his other contentions stated in the later parts of his article. The greatest departure from the Gandhian ideal, he holds, has been the pursuit of the material standards of the west by means of the western techniques of industrialization and by extreme centralization promoted by the National Planning Commission. Similarly, he further argues that India's foreign policy, though containing theoretically many elements that may be called Gandhian, has operationally been un-Gandhian in many respects. It is very difficult to say what views Gandhi would have held on these issues if he had been alive. He was, after all, concerned with the perpetual seeking after truth and designing his methods to tackle individual situations on the basis of his search. Further, the fact that power cannot be eliminated from human relations, a fact which Gandhi, as Tinker believes, recognized, has got to be taken into account. It is possible that in view of his growing realization of the importance of power politics Gandhi could have thought of a reformulation of his ideas. Besides, would it not be too much of a rash judgement to say that Gandhism has failed only because India has failed to follow Gandhi's path? Towards the end of his article Tinker himself admits that the Gandhian influence is discernible in the continuing role of compromise and consensus in Indian politics and that this role is being played by persons both inside and outside politics and administration. In the beginning of the article, however, he lays down the criterion of furtherance or non-furtherance of the tradition of compromise for determining the success or failure of Gandhism. Curiously enough he admits the role of compromise in Indian politics and yet holds that the Gandhian ideal in India has been a "magnificent failure".

Whereas the articles by Nimbark and Tinker aim at an assessment of Gandhi's current relevance, though they follow different approaches, there are two other articles which have been published recently and which are concerned with a more responsible and fundamental task of a student of peace research: that of reconstructing some of Gandhi's basic ideas into a suitable, current system of thought and action. One of these articles is "The Nature and Methods of Nonviolent Coercion"[42] by Anthony De Crespigny. This article attempts to explore the concept of coercion as a method of political activity and to evolve a satisfactory system of classifying the methods of nonviolent coercion. Nonviolent coercion is defined by Crespigny as an attempt to limit or destroy freedom of choice which does not involve the threat or use of physical force, whether directed against persons or property. This nonviolent coercion may be both direct and indirect. The author gives many examples to clarify the distinction between direct nonviolent coercion and indirect nonviolent coercion. However, the entire treatment of this eassy is centred on a discussion of the political aspect of nonviolent coercion, in the sense that its ultimate aim is to bring about or prevent a change in the policy or structure of a political government. While discussing various forms of political nonviolent coercion the author takes up boycott, strike, civil disobedience, severance of diplomatic relations, refusal to participate in elections, refusal to pay taxes, refusal to co-operate in the operation of governmental machinery, and non-cooperation. In sum, Crespigny's whole thesis is that nonviolent coercion is an attempt to limit the freedom of choice of the opponent without resort to the use of force. All forms of nonviolent coercion that he discusses have this common characteristic and whatever distinction there may be among them is only in relation to the area and circumstances of their operation. However, there are two problems regarding the concept of nonviolent coercion which he takes cognizance of but which he does not succeed in solving. The first is that

[42] Anthony De Crespigny, "The Nature and Method of Nonviolent Coercion", *Political Studies,* Vol. 12, June 1964, pp. 256-65.

of determining in specific instances when coercion has actually taken place and the second is that of determining the extent to which coercion, if it has taken place, has been effective. In this connexion it would perhaps be worth while recalling what Gandhi believed in regard to the aims of his theory of Satyagraha. Restricting the opponent's freedom of choice would, after all, be useful only when this restriction compels him to choose only the right course of action. And righteousness can come only from moral considerations. That is why Gandhi insisted on faith in Truth and in God from whom emerges morality. In any case, Crespigny's article is a scientific analysis of the concept of nonviolent coercion. It may perhaps be called a new version, re-evaluated from a critical, modern point of view, of the concept of nonviolent coercion given by C.M. Case more than forty yers ago in his *Nonviolent Coercion*, which has already been referred to in this survey.

As a matter of fact, any reinterpretation of nonviolent coercion in modern times by those interested in a systematization of peaceful techniques of resolving conflicts, particularly in the context of Gandhian philosophy, has got to concern itself with the importance of courage. A true understanding of the significance of courage in Gandhian philosophy, therefore, is necessary. It is this understanding which Susanne Hoeber Rudolph tries to give in her article "The New Courage: An Essay on Gandhi's Psychology"[43]. The political basis of Gandhi's faith in courage was his understanding of the fear of Indian people and of their scepticism about their ability to eliminate the British rule from India. Therefore, the Gandhian technique of Satyagraha had much more than strategic significance; it provided a way of action by which Indians could learn self-esteem and gain courage. According to Rudolph, the lesson of courage taught by Gandhi was particularly significant in a society like the Indian in which the distinction between the martial and the non-martial inculcated a nonviolent perspective in some cases and an aggressive one in others. The martials adhered to the British rule for political reasons and the non-martials produced nationalism. But as the nationalists lacked courage, Gandhi's task

[43] Susanne Hoeber Rudolph, "The New Courage: An Essay on Gandhi's Psychology", *World Politics* (Princeton), Vol. 16, October 1963, pp. 98-117.

was to make them courageous. But, for him, the issue of courage and cultural integrity were interconnected. Rudolph holds that Gandhi tried to solve the problem of courage and cultural integrity for himself personally but the solution he found for himself after decades of experience helped his generation as a whole and can perhaps also help the generations after him. But Gandhi's emphasis on courage did not have any contradiction with the traditional Indian belief in compromise, arbitration, and de-emphasis of overt clashes and victories or defeats — all as methods of conflict resolution. What Gandhi did was to translate these traditional Indian convictions about conflict resolution and his ideas about courage into techniques of action. Thus in finding the technique which he gave to Indian nationalism, Gandhi returned to the mild, nonviolent, but ascetic and self-suffering ethics of India. He resurrected an old and familiar path, gave it a new toughness and discipline in action, made it an effective device of mass action, and infused into it the reinvigorated content of sacrifice and self-control. In the process of getting rid of his own fear and weakness, he assured several generations of his countrymen that they need not fear those who had conquered them and that they were not cowards. Thus Rudolph's conclusion is that Gandhi taught his countrymen no new path to courage. But Gandhi never claimed to have given anything new. He was only concerned with reminding his countrymen of their past culture and genius and, as such, the courage he instilled into the people has been inherent in India's tradition itself and Gandhi was a part of that tradition.

There are yet two other admirable articles which should belong to this part of our survey. Both of them are entitled "The Future of Nonviolence". But the authors are different. One is Dave Dellinger[44] and the other is Olivier Lacombe.[45] Dellinger warns against the assumptions emanating from the unthinkability of nuclear war because he holds that nonviolence cannot be successfully used to protect special privileges that have been won by violence. He does not say, however,

[44] Dave Dellinger, "The Future of Nonviolence", *Studies on the Left* (New York), Vol. 5, Winter 1965, pp. 90-96. This article has also been reproduced in *Gandhi Marg* (New Delhi), Vol. 9, July 1965, pp. 222-28.

[45] Olivier Lacombe, "The Future of Nonviolence", in *The Emerging World*, pp. 93-96.

that there are any inherent defects in the nonviolent method.
He only asserts that nonviolence is currently incapable of resolving the problems with which mankind is faced today. By
this assertion Dellinger has reminded peace researchers of
their responsibility to devise concrete methods by which nonviolence can be made effective. In this connection Dellinger
has made a very significant observation: that the major advances
in nonviolence have not come from people who have taken nonviolence as an end in itself but from those who passionately
strove to free themselves and others from injustice. This indeed can be useful to peace researchers engaged in discovering
peaceful techniques of change. On the other hand, Lacombe
poses two questions in his article. One, whether asceticism is
relevant to civil life, if at all, in the same way as it is to personal
or religious life; and, two, whether the world society which is
increasingly becoming technological can be ordered by nonviolent methods of conflict resolution. Lacombe discusses
only the second question and not both. His answer to that question is in the affirmative. His assertion is that although we
should not be overoptimistic about the potentialities of nonviolence, efforts should be made to create conditions in which
nonviolence predominates violence. This assertion of his is
based upon his sense of history which tells him that no definite
forces work incessantly in history. Perhaps the most recent
publication on Gandhi is Giuliano Pontara's article on "The
Rejection of Violence in Gandhian Ethics of Conflict Resolution"[46]. It is devoted to the problem of Gandhi's rejection of
violence in group conflicts. Pontara not only discusses this
problem from the point of view of Gandhi's own reasons for
rejecting violence but also tries to identify situations in
which the use of violence could be permitted by
Gandhi himself. Pontara's conclusions are that Gandhi
condemned violence both because he considered it morally
bad and because it could lead only to undesirable consequences,
and that Gandhi would prefer violence in a choice between
direct violence and indirect violence or between violence and
cowardice. There is nothing new in these conclusions in so far
as they go by themselves. But the treatment of the subject

---

[46] Giuliano Fontara, "The Rejection of Violence in Gandhian Ethics of Conflict Resolution", *Journal of Peace Research*, 1965, No. 3, pp. 197-215.

and the methodology adopted for the treatment are such as they offer certain useful hypotheses for peace research. One such hypothesis could be that violence can be permissible in situations in which the avoidance of little violence is likely to result in greater violence. This hypothesis can be built up on the basis of Pontara's own finding that Gandhi expressed preference for direct violence to indirect violence. Pontara has not suggested the investigation of this hypothesis. But it is important to find out the possibility of the control of violence with the use of violence because the control of violence is the purpose of peace research.

PEACE RESEARCH AND VIOLENCE

This brings us to the question of the relationship between nonviolence and violence. We cannot be unmindful of violence as a fact of human life. For it is only by accepting violence and its efficacy that we can find out ways and means to control it and harness it to our needs. We can think of nonviolence only if we can point out how nonviolence can perform the functions which have so far been performed by violence. One such function is the resolution of intragroup and intergroup conflicts. To resolve such conflicts by nonviolent means, a thorough understanding of the nature of violence, perhaps more thorough then even the understanding of nonviolence, is necessary.

The latest and perhaps the most comprehensive and systematic study of the nature of violence is provided by a special issue of *Annals of the American Academy of Political and Social Science*.[47] The issue contains more than a dozen articles under the general theme "Patterns of Violence". Some of these articles deal with violence in the special context of America's domestic problems. But some of them are of a general theoretical nature also. Thus Marvin Wolfgang advances in his preface a thesis of a "subculture of violence" by which he means a system of norms and values set apart from the dominant nonviolent culture. This subculture of violence is based on the belief that violence can be used in

[47] "Patterns of Violence", *Arnals of the American Academy of Political and Social Science* (Philadelphia), Vol. 364, March 1966, pp. 1-248.

many kinds of social relationships. The question of what function is performed by violence is taken up by Lewis Coser in his essay "Some Social Functions of Violence". He discusses three social functions: violence as a form of achievement, violence as a danger signal, and violence as a cataclyst. Elton McNeil's "Violence and Human Development" is also a significant contribution to peace research. It makes a plea for an adequate understanding of the forces that shape the individual's attitude towards violence so that we could think of suitable ways of transforming violent attitudes into nonviolent attitudes.

While the preface-writer of the special issue of *Annals* talks of a "subculture of violence", a recently published full-length study puts forth a thesis[48] of a "culture of violence". This study is *Cultures of Violence* by Austin Porterfield. But whether we believe in a culture or a subculture of violence, the underlying assertion behind both the concepts is the same, namely that we should have a clear understanding of the nature and function of violence and that this understanding requires research into the sociological aspects of both violence and nonviolence. Peace researchers are aware of the seriousness of this requirement and quite a few of them are engaged in discovering the sociology of nonviolence. Although the results of their research are not yet published, some preliminary papers in mimeographed form are available.[49]

A book deserving special mention here is *Substitutes for Violence*[50] by John Fischer. Fischer holds that the problem before us is essentially one of devising new goals in the pursuit of which youth will find outlets for its basic instinct for action. He argues that the amenities of modern civilization have not completely stilled man's ancient instinct for action and adventure. Fischer's theory is relevant for peace research because it throws a challenge to peace researchers to discover

[48] Austin L. Porterfield, *Cultures of Violence* (Potishman, 1965).

[49] Important among such papers are Martin Oppenheimer, "Towards a Sociology of Nonviolence", Paper read at the Eastern Sociological Society, Boston, in April 1964; and T.K.N. Unnithan, "Towards a Sociology of Nonviolence", Paper read at the Inaugural Conference of the International Peace Research Association held at Groningen, the Netherlands, in July 1965. The Sixth World Congress of Sociology held in France in September 1966 took up a detailed discussion on "Sociological Aspects of the Strategy of Peace in the Atomic Age".

[50] John Fischer, *Substitutes for Violence* (New York, 1965).

alternate avenues for the expression of violence so that its destructive function can be transformed into a constructive one.

An important aspect of violence refers to various shades and manifestations of violence. In his *The Heart of Man*,[51] Erich Fromm touches this very aspect and analyses various types of violence — *playful violence, reactive violence, revengeful violence,* and *compensatory violence.* This book opens new approaches to psychoanalytical theory and dynamic social psychology by examining man's instinct of violence and nonviolence in the light of some of Freud's discoveries. But Fromm does all this ultimately to show how man may escape from "his own greatest prison — the destructive aspect of himself". Thus Fromm's book should prove immensely useful to peace researchers because the psychological approach is among the principal approaches allowed by peace researchers themselves. No less useful is the article on "Violence and the Process of Terror"[52] by E.V. Walter.

Another recent and significant study on violence is "Uses of Violence"[53] by H.L. Nieburg whose argument is that the risk of violence is necessary as well as useful in the preservation of national societies. According to Nieburg, violence has two aspects: actual use and potential use. The former would include demonstration, crimes of passion, property and politics etc., whereas the latter would mean threats. These two aspects of violence, holds Nieburg, are inextricable. He suggests that the actual demonstration of violence is necessary from time to time in order to give credibility to the threatened outbreak of violence. His assumption is that there is a dynamic process of consensus and competition involved in all kinds of human relationships. The function of conflict is to discover the consensus and in so far as demonstration of violence helps this function of conflict, violence is useful and helpful. It is from this point of view that Nieburg considers all violence as having a rational aspect for somebody or the other. In fact, the entire corpus of his argument emanates from his awareness of the functions of violence in domestic legal systems and from his

---

[51] Erich Fromm, *The Heart of Man* (London, 1965).
[52] E.V. Walter, "Violence and the Process of Terror", *American Sociological Review* (Washington, D.C.), Vol. 29, April 1964, pp. 248-57.
[53] H.L. Nieburg, "Uses of Violence", *Journal of Conflict Resolution,* Vol. 7, March 1963, pp. 43-54.

belief that violence has the same function to perform in the international sphere as it has in the domestic sphere. That is why he thinks that there is no choice possible between law and violence and almost ridicules the efforts of international lawyers and world governmentalists to eliminate war. Rather he believes that the threat of violence tends to create stability and maintain peace because the dangers of a minor international conflict escalating into a major one induce greater restraint on the part of national leaders in their relations with each other. That the use of force has some function to perform in the domestic sphere cannot be denied. But the evolution of a nonviolent social order entails the gradual reduction in dependence upon force. Therefore, it does not matter whether nonviolence is successful in one or in all cases. The purpose should be to try to enlarge the area of the application of nonviolence. Nieburg is right when he says that the strategy of nonviolent social action does not preclude the threat of force as an instrument of social change. But in saying so he concerns himself with the situation as it exists and not with how violence could be replaced by nonviolence which, in fact, is a more important problem. Whatever be the merits or demerits of Nieburg's paper, his contention that the threat of violence, not its actual use, is necessary and useful, is significant for problems of peace research. For it is possible that further research might indicate ways and means by which the threatened use of violence could be developed into an effective component of the technique of nonviolence. Another question, that Nieburg's analysis raises, concerns the relationship between his contention and the deterrence theory of international politics.

In his "Reflections on Violence"[54] Herbert Read contends that we must accept violence and believe in its ultimate efficacy. This may sound unacceptable. But on reading the whole paper carefully one should realize that even this contention, if read with Read's line of reasoning, can be helpful in the development of the power of nonviolence. Read holds that violence is a component of the evolutionary process. But this does not mean that we should condone it. On the contrary,

[54] Herbert Read, "Reflections on Violence", in *The Emerging World*, n. 36, pp. 170-73.

our attempt should be to control this force and harness it to our needs so that we are able to preserve that nonviolent mode of life which Read calls civilization. According to Read, even Gandhi's nonviolence is the recognition of the reality of violence. That is why Gandhi preached its control. Thus nonviolent resistance, in his view, is nothing else but the continued control of violence and that constitutes the explanation of its effectiveness. All this may be unpalatable. But the logic of the argument is not unsound. For, if we recognize the reality of violence, we can perhaps work harder and make greater efforts for the transformation of violence and thus brighten the prospects of peace.

While Nieburg and Read examine the role of violence in a theoretical context, Robert Williamson does the same thing in a particular practical context of rural Colombia. In his "Toward A Theory of Political Violence"[55], he tries to apply the existing theories of violence as an aspect of social conflict and then examines those theories in the light of the experiences of rural Colombia. In so doing he points out possibilities of the evolution of a theory defining proper relationship between violence and nonviolence.

It should be pointed out, however, that the arguments of Read or Nieburg about the usefulness of violence should not be taken as a plea for the justification of war. In fact, it is necessary now, more than ever before, to make people aware of the threat of war and particularly of the horrors of thermonuclear extermination on the one hand and to find out ways of averting those threats and horrors on the other. Two important studies in this connexion are *Breakthrough to Peace*[56] and *Preventing World War III: Some Proposals*[57], both of which are edited volumes. The former contains twelve papers representing different points of view about the destructiveness of thermonuclear war and written by distinguished scholars like Norman Cousins, Erich Fromm, Lewis Mumford, Walter Stein, Thomas Morton, and others. A common

[55] Robert C. Williamson, "Toward A Theory of Political Violence", *Western Political Quarterly*, Vol. 18, March 1965, pp. 35-44.
[56] New Directions Books, *Breakthrough to Peace* (Norfolk, Connecticut, 1962).
[57] Quincy Wright, William M. Evan, and Morton Deutsch, eds., *Preventing World War III: Some Proposals* (New York, 1962).

feature of all the papers in this volume is that their perspectives are essentially humanistic. They look beyond the restricted interests of any particular group towards the most crucial need of mankind, that is, peace. One essay that deserves special mention is "Breaking the Thought Barrier: Psychological Challenges of the Nuclear Age" by Jerome D. Frank. After giving a review of the dangers of nuclear weapons, which is rather sketchy, the author puts forth the contention that the psychological challenge of the nuclear age is to find out means of persuasion which may be more effective than violence and to create conditions in which the wielder of power is inhibited from using it. For this, he thinks, breaking the existing thought barrier is absolutely necessary. Frank examines the relevance of nonviolence in this connexion and concludes that nonviolence can break this thought barrier. In so doing he also tries to remove some of the common misunderstandings about nonviolence, including the one that reliance on nonviolence requires complete elimination of conflict. According to him, one important reason for the ineffectiveness of what he calls "pacifist preachments" is that we regard them as hopelessly idealistic and view human nature as essentially aggressive and self-aggrandizing. But on the basis of a brief study of the essence of nonviolent campaigns he strikes a note of optimism when he states that there is a possibility of mankind's subscribing to values which exclude war. He also refers to the contributions of Gandhi and Martin Luther King to nonviolence, and also to the lessons that could be derived from this experience. In particular, he points out two cautions: that in the case of both Gandhi and King the use of nonviolence was in an intrasocietal and not intersocietal setting; and that in each case society was grounded in democratic values. He hopes, nevertheless, that nonviolence can be successful even in an intersocietal setting and also in a non-democratic society. But how could it be possible is a question that is left to the readers to answer for themselves. He only says towards the end of his paper that "the most likely source of conversion of mankind to renunciation of mass violence would be a nuclear accident which would bring home the horrors of modern war". This statement is obviously based upon the assumption, although Frank does not say so in clear terms, that if the two world wars have shaken man's faith in force and have compelled him to think of nonviolence, a nuclear war would give man complete faith in nonviolence.

While *Breakthrough to Peace* introduces to the readers the various types of threats of nuclear war, *Preventing World War III* evokes thinking and makes suggestions about how to reduce the dangers of those threats. The book is divided into two parts, one dealing with methods of stopping the arms race and the other with those of reducing international tensions. As a whole, the book covers a variety of aspects connected with the problems of war and peace.

CONFLICT AND VIOLENCE

However, peace research has to establish relationship not merely between violence and nonviolence but also between violence and conflict. Peace research is essentially a discipline which has emerged as a result of man's effort to apply sociological theories to problems of war and peace. An important study that should be mentioned in this connexion is *The Nature of Conflict: Studies of the Sociological Aspects of International Tensions*,[58] published by the Unesco. The contributors to this volume are Jessie Bernard, T.H. Pear, Raymond Aron, and Robert Angell. It does not presume that conflict can be eliminated from human society. Rather it believes in the inevitability of conflict. The task of peace research is to see how conflict can be resolved peacefully. Thus peace research is based upon a belief in the futility of violence as a means of conflict resolution and on a hope that an alternative to violence can be found out. Research based on this belief and this hope should naturally be concerned with two fundamental questions: what are the bases of a belief in the futility of violence? and what are the causes, nature, and functions of conflict. An answer to the first question has been attempted in recent studies like *Alternatives to War and Violence*,[59] edited by Ted Dunn, "Violence and Hostility: The

---

[58] Unesco, *The Nature of Conflict: Studies in the Sociological Aspects of International Tensions* (Paris, 1957).

[59] Ted Dunn, ed., *Alternatives to War and Violence* (London, 1964).

Path to World War"[60] by Ole Holsti, Richard Brody, and Robert North, and *Instead of Violence*[61], edited by A. and L. Weinberg. Of these three, the volume edited by Dunn is most comprehensive. According to Dunn, violence may also be non-lethal, that is, one which is done to the body. But this may be reversible. In Dunn's volume, chapters by Gene Sharp and Anthony Weaver are especially relevant. Anthony Weaver has also brought out an independent publication, under the title *War Outmoded — as a Method of Settling Disputes: A Guide to Thought and Action*,[62] which discusses, among other things, nonviolent resistance and Satyagraha.

The second question, what are the functions, nature and causes of conflict?, is also relevant to peace research. There is inexhaustible material dealing with this question. But the present survey is concerned with only those items which are recent and which reflect an attempt to reexamine the nature and function of conflict with the objective of finding out how conflict can be dealt with in a way conducive to peace. Two such items are *Conflict and Defense*[63] by Kenneth Boulding and *International Conflict and Behaviour Science*[64] edited by R. Fisher. Boulding's conviction is that we must study conflict as a general social process and study war as a special case of that process. With this conviction Boulding develops an integral theory of conflict as a dynamic social process and applies it to various fields of social life — economic, industrial, international, ideological, and ethical. Contributors to Fisher's edited volume have also examined the various facets of conflict from a sociological point of view and with the help of the approach of the behavioural science. An interesting essay included in Fisher's volume is "Toward a Theory of Peace"[65] by Kenneth Boulding.

In his essay on "New Directions in Research on Conflict

---

[60] Ole R. Holsti, Richard A. Brody, and Robert C. North, "Violence and Hostility: The Path to World War", mimeographed.
[61] Arthur and Lila Weinberg, eds., *Instead of Violence* (New York, 1963).
[62] Anthony Weaver, *War Outmoded—as a Method of Settling Disputes: A Guide to Thought and Action* (London, 1960). For the relevant portion see pp. 38-59.
[63] Kenneth E. Boulding, *Conflict and Defense: A General Theory* (New York, 1962).
[64] R. Fisher, ed., *International Conflict and Behaviour Science* (New York, 1964).
[65] Kenneth E. Boulding, "Toward a Theory of Peace", in *Ibid.*, pp. 70-87.

Resolution"[66] Kenneth Hammond points out the changing nature of conflict. He believes that the world has nearly reached a stage where there is a recognition of common problems. But this recognition marks a change in the nature of conflict. Earlier we had conflict over ends but agreement about means; but now we have agreement about the end — peace and survival — but conflict over means. Hammond envisages that in the next decade or so peace would be threatened not by the absence of commonly recognized end but by disagreement about the means to ensure peace. He calls this disagreement cognitive conflict. His purpose in this article, therefore, is to stimulate research efforts to uncover information about cognitive conflict and its resolution. This is Hammond's personal view which relates to future possibilities. But scholars in general are not yet prepared to agree that nations have solved the problem of identifying their joint interests and common values. Research on conflict is only beginning to show that there are certain principles concerning the relationship between conflict and violence[67] and that it is possible to contain conflict in such a way that it does not break out in organized violence. Aside from the question whether or not there is a recognition of common interests, the problem of cognitive conflict is important. For there are various approaches that have been suggested in recent years for the containment of conflict. A critical examination of these approaches is available in "New Roads To A World Without War"[68] by Arthur Waskow. Waskow first discusses new ideas on the nature of conflict and ethics of violence and then examines various proposals for the control of conflict. Two other essays that should fit in this part of the survey are "Conflict and Power in Society"[69] by Emanuel de Kadt and "The Turn

[66] Kenneth R. Hammond, "New Directions in Research on Conflict Resolution", *Journal of Social Issues* (Worcester, Mass.), Vol. 21, July 1965, pp. 44-66.

[67] It is reported that Arthur I. Waskow has recently completed a study on *A Study in the Connections Between Conflict and Violence* which is expected to be published soon.

[68] Arthur I. Waskow, "New Roads To A World Without War", Yale Review (New Haven), Vol. 54, October 1964, pp. 85-111.

[69] Emanuel J. de Kadt, "Conflict and Power in Society", *International Social Science Journal*, Vol. 17, No. 3, 1965, pp. 454-71.

Toward Peace"[70] by D.F. Fleming. One would also find useful *The Nature of Human Conflict*[71] edited by Elton McNeil and *Dimensions of Conflict Within Nations, 1955-60: Turmoil and Internal War*[72] by Raymond Tanter.

A special issue of the Journal called *Inquiry,* published by the Oslo University Press and devoted to a symposium on "Peace and Conflict", is also of great value. The issue contains several papers[73] dealing with the nature of relationship between peace and conflict. Actually the significance of sociological study of conflict and its relation with peace is being increasingly realized. The international symposium on "Conflict in Society", held in London in July 1965 under the sponsorship of the Ciba Foundation and another symposium on "Causes of Conflicts" held in Rome in September 1965 under the sponsorship of World Academy of Arts and Science reflect the realization of this significance. The papers presented at the London Symposium have been published in the form of a book under the title *Conflict in Society*.[74]

PEACE RESEARCH AND
INTERNATIONAL RELATIONS

Peace research is closely connected with international relations. For the realization of the objectives of peace research depends upon the evolution of peaceful international relations. Peace research, therefore, views international relations from an absolutely fresh, non-traditional angle.

---

[70] D.F. Fleming, "The Turn Toward Peace", *Annals,* Vol. 351, January 1964, pp. 157-69.
[71] Elton B. McNeil, ed., *The Nature of Human Conflict* (Ann Arbor, 1965).
[72] Raymond Tanter, *Dimensions of Conflict Within Nations, 1955-60: Turmoil and Internal War* (New York, 1965).
[73] Chief among them are: "Roots of Conflict and Action" by K. Aschenbrenner; "Ethics and Responsibility in Politics" by Gene Sharp; and "The Significance of Unasked Questions in the Study of Conflict" by P.B. Hume and Joan V. Bondurant. Vide *Inquiry* (Oslo), Autumn 1964.
[74] Ciba Foundation, *Conflict in Society* (London, 1966). Important among the papers in this book are: "Conflict in Primate Society", S.L. Washburn; "Intra-Personal Conflict and the Authoritarian Character", H.V. Dicks; "Conflict in Cities", R. Glass; "Conflict in Formal Organizations", J. Van Doorn; "Conflict Management as a Learning Process", Kenneth E. Boulding; "The Role of International Law in Solving Conflicts", B.V.A. Roling; "Conflict and Leadership", Harold D. Lasswell; "The Nature of International Society", Karl W. Deutsch; "Internal and External Sources of International Tension", K. Lapter; and "Conflict as a Means of Change", John W. Burton.

Stephen King-Hall's *Power Politics in the Nuclear Age*[74] is a significant contribution in that direction.

The question King-Hall tries to answer is which type of defence would be really effective in an age of what he calls "nuclear violence". After discussing in the first part the nature of present-day international society *vis-a-vis* the development of nuclear weapons, King-Hall draws the conclusion that Great Britain should abandon the use of nuclear energy for military purposes. The author combines in himself wide experiences of a journalist, a military officer, and an independent member of Parliament. That is why the writes with great persuasion on even defence problems which are also political problems. Though his advice, that is, the abandonment of nuclear energy for military purposes, is for Great Britain, it can well serve as a guide to other nations as well. It is based on King-Hall's assumption that with the development of nuclear power there has been a simultaneous development of what he terms "nonviolent power" and that the most important element of this power is the influence of mass public opinion. The author devotes a full chapter to an analysis of the development of this power during the last half a century or so. The development of this power itself makes it easier for nations, in his view, to renounce war and go ahead with a programme of unilateral nuclear disarmament. While all that King-Hall says in this connexion is significant, his contention that Great Britain should abandon the military use of nuclear energy, not only for the sake of mankind but also for the nationalistic reasons of once more becoming a great power, raises the question as to how far the attainment of big-power status can or should be an objective for a people concerned primarily with everlasting peace. King-Hall does not take up this question in a proper perspective but his treatment certainly indicates an important avenue for research.

As a matter of fact, familiarity with the historical development of the peace movement puts peace studies of any kind in a proper perspective. That is why a publication of the Carnegie Endowment for International Peace, *Perspectives on Peace*[76],

---

[75] Stephen King-Hall, *Power Politics in the Nuclear Age* (London, 1962).
[76] Carnegie Endowmwnet for International Peace, *Perspectives on Peace* (London, 1960).

is very useful. This volume contains papers by eminent statesmen and leaders of public opinion that have played an admirable role in their search for peace. The contributors include persons like James Shotwell, Harold Nicolson, Dag Hammarskjoeld, Norman Angell, Salvador de Madariaga, and Max Huber. All the papers are in the nature of a retrospect of the efforts made for peace during the 1910-60 period and an examination of recent developments against a background of interwar experiences. The book, as such, is a cooperative attempt at a re-examination of the meaning of peace in the context of the revolutionary changes in the conditions of man's existence in the present century. Special mention should be made here of James Shotwell's thought-provoking essay entitled "Reflections on War and Peace". Its significance lies in an observation and a conclusion. The observation is that the peace movement never became a vital force in national policies before the nature of war underwent a radical change as a result of the impact of science; and the conclusion is that peace requires the substitution of international processes for war and also the strengthening of those processes.

In his *The Human Dimension in International Relations*,[77] Otto Klineberg draws attention to the fact that fear plays a causative role in the build-up of armaments and that it is fear which is the basis of the supposition that war is often justified as a defence against supposed undesirable intentions. It is Klineberg's conclusion that the removal of fear is easier among children than among adults. He suggests certain methods by which international relations could be improved and difficulties arising from fear could be solved to a certain extent. As the future of peace will depend upon the children of today, Klineberg's suggestion to infuse among children the value of peace is very sound. How it can be done is a problem whose solution requires a prior investigation into how attitudes of war and peace are formed. An article worth nothing in this connexion is "The Development of the Concept of War"[78] by Peter Cooper. The title should not mislead the

---

[77] Otto Klineberg, *The Human Dimension in International Relations* (New York, 1964).

[78] Peter Cooper, "The Development of the Concept of War", *Journal of Peace Research*, 1965, No. 1, pp. 1-17.

reader into thinking that it deals with a historical development of the concept of war. Rather it discusses the development of the attitude to war among a few hundred selected school children. On the basis of this sample survey the author has proposed certain hypotheses which are useful for further inquiry.

In any case, the development of peace attitudes among children is indeed necessary because that would prepare future statesmen who could formulate their policies in accordance with the demands of peace. This does not, however, mean that nothing should be done to influence the present national policies. How this influence should be exerted is the theme of Arthur Waskow's *The Worried Man's Guide to World Peace*[79] and B. Landheer's *Ethical Values in International Decision-Making*.[80] Waskow makes a review of peace policies and activities, suggests a set of criteria by which they can be judged, and recommends ways in which findings in social science research can be effective in influencing national policies. On the other hand, Landheer makes a powerful plea for due consideration to be paid to essential ethical values in the formulation of policies. But the formulation of peace-oriented policies which Waskow and Landheer recommend requires a new approach to power as an instrument of foreign policy. This new approach is emphasized in *Peace: The Control of National Power*[81] by Philip Van Slyck. In the context of the formation of peace attitudes, there is a very useful article recently published by Yasumasa Kuroda under the title "Correlates of the Attitudes Toward Peace".[82]

Since peace research views international relations in a perspective different from the traditional one, it is obviously concerned with a reinterpretation of various concepts and their content. War, peace, and diplomacy may be counted among such concepts. There are a large number of publications on the changed nature of war. But the most recent

[79] Arthur I. Waskow, *The Worried Man's Guide to World Peace* (New York, 1965).

[80] B. Landheer, *Ethical Values in International Decision-Making* (The Hague, 1960).

[81] Philip Van Slyck, *Peace: The Control of National Power* (Boston, 1963).

[82] Yasumasa Kuroda, "Correlates of the Attitudes Toward Peace", *Background* (Los Angeles), Vol. 8, November 1964, pp. 205-220.

ones are: "Commentary on War Since 1942"[83] by Quincy Wright, "The Nature of War"[84] by Edmund Leach, and "The Changing Phenomenon of War Since the Peace of Westphalia"[85] by F.C. Spits. Quincy Wright examines the impact of technological change and nuclear development on the nature of war and analyses the relationship which war has with balance of power and international organization. Leach discusses some of the non-rational causes of war. It is his conviction that the decision to go to war is not always possible to be governed wholly by reason. The author draws on anthropological insights to illuminate hypotheses about the motivations of war in both primitive and advanced societies. As for the causes of war, no serious study focussing on a fresh approach has appeared in recent years. But an admirable piece is available on a re-assessment of the concept of just war. It is "Contemporary Significance of the Doctrine of Just War"[86] by Lynn Miller. Needless to say that as a result of the emergence of a new system of international relations replacing the balance of power system and the tremendous increase in the destructiveness of modern weapons, the doctrine of just war has received renewed attention. Miller's article seeks to determine the extent to which the doctrine of just war may claim its relevance today and the analysis here follows a multi-dimensional approach combining disciplines of history, politics, and law. The treatment here is primarily theoretical. The contemporary significance that Miller sees in the just war doctrine is that it can be "stood on its head" so that it may be used as a proof not of the justice of a cause but of the threat to security which requires community action. The author opines that the just war theory is suffering from a crisis, resulting from the question whether resort to war (even to a just war) is preferable to peace, howsoever unjust it may be deemed. Everybody, of course, condemns resort to war but nobody is sure about what should follow in response to an act of violence. Miller's contri-

---

[83] Quincy Wright, "Commentary on War Since 1942", in his *A Study of War* (Chicago, 1965) pp. 1501-38.
[84] Edmund Leach, "The Nature of War", *Disarmament and Arms Control* (London), Vol. 3, Spring 1965, pp. 165-83.
[85] F.C. Spits. "The Changing Phenomenon of War Since the Peace of Westphalia".
[86] Lynn H. Miller, "Contemporary Significance of the Doctrine of Just War", *World Politics,* Vol. 16, January 1964, pp. 254-86.

bution lies in his assertion that we should try to prevent the just cause from occurring so that a situation demanding the use of force on "just" bases never arises and the dilemma of how to react to the use of force no longer bothers us. Another significant point he makes is that the responsibility of deciding the justness or unjustness of a cause for resort to war should rest not with individual men or nations but with an international organization like the United Nations. Robert Tucker's *The Just War*[87] examines the limits of a defensive war. Although it is a commentary on the limits of a defensive war in the American context, it raises certain perennial moral issues which are relevant even to a defensive war.

However, there has been a tendency to concern ourselves with only the causes of war and not with the causes of peace. But wars may result not only from factors inherent in a war situation but also from the absence of factors safeguarding peace. This is the belief which lies behind Werner Levi's article "On Causes of Peace"[88]. Levi's attempt in this article is to make a comparative study of those nations in which peace has been most nearly achieved and then to find out why there is a fair assurance of peace in them. These findings can be used, holds Levi, for a further investigation, that is, why there is a frequent likelihood of war in international society. It is his contention that peace within nations is not preserved by the elimination of violence or donflict. It is preserved because force is not available to the citizen and thus he is compelled to develop and strengthen peaceful means for the resolution of conflicts. The behaviour pattern of the citizen is so modelled that it discounts violence. But in the international society peace and the welfare of all do not rank among the people's highest values. Further, there is a social organization and social policy planning within nations, whereas the international society lacks any central decision-making apparatus. Again, international society is mainly political and does not develop beyond that realm. This politicization of international society hinders the development of a "system of

---

[87] Robert W. Tucker, *The Just War* (Baltimore, 1960).
[88] Werner Levi, "On Causes of Peace", *Journal of Conflict Resolution*, Vol. 8, March 1964, pp. 23-35. More than two decades ago, Edward Hallett Carr wrote a useful book explaining what is peace and what are the requirements for its achievement. See his *Conditions of Peace* (New York, 1942).

mutualities". Levi holds that for the preservation of international peace is required an international structure which tolerates conflicts and provides nonviolent institutions for their resolution and that the interdependent groups should be sufficiently large. But at present the organization of force in international society does not correspond to this requirement. The two essential conditions of international peace, then, are: the development of a behaviour pattern which denounces war and violence, and the peaceful organization of international force. Levi suggests a comprehensive programme for the achievement of these conditions. He emphasizes that this programme should be followed in nonpolitical fields. This is exactly what Gandhi also emphasized; that peace is a matter of all aspects of life and not only of the political aspect.

Mention should be made here of another article by Werner Levi, namely "The Concept of Integration in Research on Peace"[89]. In this article, Levi discusses some important issues involved in defining the concept of integration in a framework necessitated by the requirements of peace.

Irving Horowitz opines in his *The Idea of War and Peace in Contemporary Philosophy*[90] that the pacifist philosophy examines things in terms of abstract motives and that it reaches *a priori* judgement without concrete appraisal of war in the context of changing nature of society. F. Van Heek, on the other hand, has examined war from a sociological point of view in his "The Sociological Aspects of War"[91].

The emergence of a desirable pattern of international relations conducive to the objectives of peace research also requires a change in the traditional methods of international politics. In his admirable article on "Summit Meetings and International Relations"[92], therefore, Johan Galtung examines the place which summit meetings occupy in the conduct of international relations. He argues that a reduction in or complete cancellation of summit meetings can prove to be a

[89] Werner Levi, "The Concept of Integration in Research on Peace", *Background* (Los Angeles), Vol. 9, August 1965, pp. 111-26.
[90] Irving L. Horowitz, *The Idea of War and Peace in Contemporary Philosophy* (New York, 1957).
[91] F. Van Heek, "The Sociological Aspects of War", *International Journal of Comparative Sociology* (Toronto), Vol. 5, March 1964, pp. 25-39.
[92] Johan Galtung, "Summit Meetings and International Relations", *Journal of Peace Research*, No. 1, 1964, pp. 36-54.

meaningful and useful sanction in a conflict. This principle corresponds in substance to the principle of nonviolent non-cooperation, inasmuch a nation reducing the level of summit meetings or cancelling them would do so with the obvious object of announcing its unwillingness to cooperate with any nation that threatens peace. It does not mean that there should be no contact among those nations among whom summit meetings are suspended. Galtung suggests that even during such suspension, there should be institutionalized meetings within the neutral framework provided by the United Nations so that permanent needs for contact and agreement may be satisfied. However, the definition of a summit meeting given by Galtung is rather narrow. He defines "summit meeting" as an *ad hoc* meeting in which heads of state or government or foreign ministers of at least two big powers are present. If the principle of non-cooperation is to be applied in international relationships, this application can contribute to prospects of peace only if it works at the highest possible level of generality. In that case Galtung's definition of a summit meeting will have to be revised so as to cover all official meetings between one nation(s) and another nation(s). It is only by enlarging its scope that international non-cooperation can be developed into an effecive technique.

The utility of the study of the structure of diplomacy to peace research is obvious. In their article, entitled "Patterns of Diplomacy"[93], Johan Galtung and Mari Holmboe Ruge make an interesting study of diplomacy in terms of its main functions—negotiation and representation—and as a channel of information. A number of hypotheses have been advanced about how diplomacy changes under the impact of growing internationalization. The authors also make some predictions with regard to the future form of diplomacy as also with regard to sources of conflict in future. One such prediction is that bilateral diplomacy would soon fall into discredit, that it would be considered a sign of hostility rather than of friendship, and that it would be replaced by multilateral diplomacy

---

[93] Johan Galtung and Mari Holmboe Ruge, "Patterns of Diplomacy", *Journal of Peace Research*, No. 2, 1965, pp. 101-35. Another article worth noting in this connexion is Suzanne Keller, "Diplomacy and Communication", *Public Opinion Quarterly* (Princeton), Vol. 20, pp. 176-82.

and other institutions of multi-international contact.

PEACE RESEARCH AND DISARMAMENT AND ARMS CONTROL

Disarmament and arms control are the important problems that characterize the present phase of international politics and the solution of these problems falls within the scope of peace research. Innumerable books and articles have been published on these problems. But most of them deal with the strategic, technical, historical, and legal aspects. Let it be stressed, therefore, that the survey in this section is not concerned with those studies on disarmament and arms control which have been made with a view to formulating strategies and with a political bias. Here we are concerned with those most recent publications on disarmament which either reflect a peace research approach or deal with the latest phase of the problem of arms control, namely non-proliferation of nuclear weapons. An important aspect of the relationship between peace research and disarmament is the relationship between armers and disarmers. David Singer holds in his *Deterrence, Arms Control, and Disarmament*[94] that there is need for a serious study of military strategy because it contributes to the "professionalization" of the peace worker and makes it possible for policy discussions to be conducted in a language that is familiar to both civilians and military policy-makers. Anatol Rapoport, on the other hand, rejects in his *Strategy and Conscience*[95] the possibility of a genuine debate between military men and the peace workers because he does not concede the reciprocity of influence. In his *Peace and Opinion*,[96] Evan Luard analyses some of the difficulties encountered in the achievement of disarmament and arms control. He tries to show that efforts for disarmament made so far are directed to symptoms, rather than to the causes, of international disorder. He, therefore, suggests what he calls political disarmament which could be possible, in his view, under the pressure of in-

---

[94] J. David Singer, *Deterrence, Arms Control, and Disarmament* (Ohio, 1962).
[95] Anatol Rapoport, *Strategy and Conscience* (New York, 1964).
[96] Evan Luard, *Peace and Opinion* (London, 1962).

ternational public opinion against arms race. Seymour Melman has given the idea of "peace race" as a substitute for arms race. His monograph, *The Peace Race*,[97] makes a plea for diverting the resources in the direction of world industrialization with freedom, disarmament, and international cooperation. More or less the same idea pervades throughout the argument developed by Amitai Etzioni in his *Winning Without War*[98]. Etzioni holds that the best way for the United States to win "war" with the Soviet Union is to compete with her successfully in assisting the development programmes of underdeveloped countries. Another contribution made by Amitai Etzioni is "Forum: War, Peace, and the Uncommitteed Nations"[99]. The idea of peace race has been recently applied by Paul Smoker in his article "Sino-Indian Relations: A Study of Trade, Communication, and Defence"[100]. First of all Smoker examines the nature of relationship between the two countries. The conclusion drawn is that India pursued a nonviolent defence policy during the period up to 1962, because during this period India tried to meet the increased tension by reducing defence expenditure and increasing communication. But after 1962, holds Smoker, India developed faith in the principle of security through military strength. This transformation of India's policy from nonviolent to military defence offers an interesting case study for peace research. For peace research is after all concerned with the prevention of such a transformation, which is possible only with the help of a proper study of the factors contributing to this transformation. Smoker's view is that the change in India's policy came as a result of the failure of communications system between India and China and, hence, he recommends the development of peace race. Smoker further develops this recommendation in another article "Fear in the Arms Race: A Mathematical Study"[101] and it is relevant not only to Sino-Indian relations but to the whole complex of international

[97] Seymour Melman, *The Peace Race* (New York, 1962).
[98] Amitai Etzioni, *Winning Without War* (New York, 1964).
[99] Amitai Etzioni, "Forum: War, Peace, and the Uncommitteed Nations", *Social Research*, Vol. 31, Spring 1964, pp. 126-27.
[100] Paul Smoker, "Sino-Indian Relations: A Study of Trade, Communication, and Defence", *Journal of Peace Research*, No. 2, 1964, pp. 65-76.
[101] Paul Smoker, "Fear in the Arms Race: A Mathematical Study", *Journal of Peace Research*, No. 1, 1964, pp. 55-64.

relations. The underlying assumption behind this theory is that the deterrence theory as the basis of foreign policies only makes war more probable by accelerating the process of arms race. It is during the small periods of relaxation or what Lewis Richardson[102] calls periods of submissiveness that decision-makers should try their best to keep the system going in the direction of disarmament. Positive peace measures like elite communication and cultural exchanges should be undertaken during these periods. Such measures will be the steps in peace race. As a matter of fact, the theory of peace race is itself based upon the realization of the need for an effective communications system because peace race can contribute to the prospects of disarmament and check arms race only if the intentions of those making a start in peace race are not misunderstood.

Perhaps the most serious problem engaging the attention of the world today is to check the spread of nuclear weapons. *The Dispersion of Nuclear Weapons: Strategy and Politics,*[103] edited by R.N. Rosecrance, aims at discussing this very problem. It is a collection of papers by seven scholars of the Rand Corporation. Points of view of various countries, especially those of great powers, to the problem of the spread of nuclear weapons are examined. All the contributors seem to be unanimous in their assumption that the world would be quite happy if there were only a bipolar nuclear monopoly between the Soviet Union and the United States. Although such a situation would be preferable to the impending danger of the dispersion of nuclear weapons, it is doubtful if world public opinion would be satisfied with the retention of the bipolar nuclear monopoly as a permanent feature of international life. For the acceptance of this situation implies a prior acceptance of the assumption that ideological orientation is the chief motive force in international relations. In any case, the problem of the dispersion of nuclear weapons is closely related to the problem of disarmament, inasmuch as the solution of the one cannot be imagined without the solution or at least the hope of a solution of the other. Therefore,

---

[102] See Lewis F. Richardson, *Arms and Insecurity* (London, 1960).
[103] R.N. Rosecrance, ed., *The Dispersion of Nuclear Weapons* (New York, 1964).

First Steps to Disarmament,[104] edited by Evan Luard, has relevance here. It covers a wide field, ranging from the history of disarmament negotiations to the problem of verification in arms control. The onus of the argument is that the failure in disarmament efforts has been due to the fact that every time very comprehensive documents have been produced to achieve disarmament. As such, a suggestion is made in this book that less comprehensive agreements in restricted fields of disarmament should be the aim now. Experts in the field of disarmament and arms control discuss a number of such restricted measures as can help ensure some degree of success. These measures are called first steps towards disarmament. In the conclusion, written by Evan Luard himself, the need for recognizing the factors that may affect disarmament efforts in future is emphasized. Among the steps suggested to be taken immediately are the non-proliferation of nuclear weapons, institutionalization of the means to find out the balancing military strength of all nations, and the evolution of an effective inspection system. Another book that must be noted in this context is *Disarmament and International Law*[105] by Allan Gotlieb. Though the focus of the book is legal, it makes an excellent analysis of the political aspect too, inasmuch as the relationship between disarmament and international law is seen in the light of political conditions. It is Gotlieb's contention that the development of international law and the conclusion of a disarmament treaty should go together as parts of a single process. In holding this view, the author rightly emphasizes the fact that disarmament can be effective only when we have workable means for the peaceful settlement of international disputes. That is why he underlines the need for the institutionalization of already existing peaceful means for the resolution of conflicts, a need which peace research also takes note of. It is this need which is the subject matter of international law and which provides the relationship between international law and disarmament. Further, the relevance of this relationship arises from the fact of national sovereignty which often impedes the implementation of peace plans. So much so that international law remains the only hope during dis-

[104] Evan Luard, ed., *First Steps to Disarmament* (London, 1965).
[105] Allan Gotlieb, *Disarmament and International Law* (Toronto, 1965).

armament negotiations because it alone can sanction peace-keeping functions of the international community and thus help the growth of the concept of peaceful change.

Must the Bomb Spread?[106] by Leonard Beaton is also an excellent study on the subject. The author outlines a political strategy of allaying the motives of security and prestige that are making some countries inclined towards nuclear policies. He suggests that the prestige attached to the possession of nuclear weapons must wane. He also opines that the nuclear guarantee by nuclear powers to non-nuclear countries already exists in some measure in the policies of great powers. On the whole, this book presents the idea of a "non-proliferation system". It conveys, with confidence and firmness, some of Beaton's ideas which were put only as tentative propositions in his earlier book *The Spread of Nuclear Weapons*[107] which Beaton wrote with John Maddox.

In fact, the problem of both dispersion of nuclear weapons and disarmament has arisen from the phenomenal technological advancement which, on the one hand, has enriched physical life and, on the other, has created a crisis of values. The first is the subject matter of *The Age of Automation*[108] by Leon Bagrit and the second is the theme of *The Technological Society*[109] by Jacques Ellul. The first book, containing the BBC Reith Lectures for 1964, underlines the author's belief that automation can radically transform the whole world in the next few decades. Bagrit discounts the fears of those who believe that automation would damage the moral worth of the individual. Such fears, in his opinion, are based upon ignorance. On the contrary, Bagrit holds that automation would bring about a world characterized by freedom from the drudgery of work, availability of enough resources to help the underdeveloped areas, and leisure for the growth of cultural values. Bagrit's lectures do not stop at painting a picture of a world society dominated by automation. He also takes up the wider question of how problems of education, political considerations, and industrial and economic consequences would be adjusted

---

[106] Leonard Beaton, *Must the Bomb Spread?* (London, 1966).
[107] Leonard Beaton and John Maddox, *The Spread of Nuclear Weapons* (London, 1962).
[108] Leon Bagrit, *The Age of Automation* (London, 1965).
[109] Jacques Ellul, *The Technological Society* (Knopf., 1964).

in the age of automation in such a way that the ultimate objective of international peace is not thwarted. Jacques Ellul touches the problem of the conflict between technical means and human values, which has arisen as a result of the technological revolution. The writer's contention is that technology is not reconcilable with individual freedom and that the conflict between technology and moral values is unresolvable. But it is difficult to accept this position. Actually, freedom itself is not possible without technology. History also testifies to the fact that pre-technical societies were closed societies. The technological advance has brought about a great accommodation between the interstices of society and the freedom of the individual.

An interesting article worth noting in this part of our survey is "The Arming of an International Police"[110] by A.C. Nunn. The subject of international police has been examined by scholars from various points of view. But Nunn points out an absolutely new dimension of the subject, inasmuch as he conceives of the possibility of an international police waging a war without killing, mutilation, or destruction of property. The method suggested by him for removing the undesirable features of war is non-lethal violence. He recommends that such an international police should function under the United Nations which should work out the details of the strategy of non-lethal violence. If it could be made to work, Nunn's suggestion is indeed valuable because it points out a way by which war could be tamed as an acceptable mode of resolving conflicts without involving destruction of men and property, thus contributing to the basic purpose of peace research.

TECHNIQUE OF PEACEFUL RESISTANCE

This takes us from the theory to the technique part of peace research. The nonviolent technique as applied by Gandhi in India and South Africa cannot be a set technique capable of successful operation in all circumstances. Therefore, the problem is to find out a new technique which may be relevant today. As this problem, like the problem of evolving a scientific

[110] A.C. Nunn, "The Arming of an International Police", *Journal of Peace Research,* 1965, No. 2, pp. 187-91.

typology of violence and nonviolence, is a problem of reconstruction, one has to consider what literature is available to provide the data for such a reconstruction. This type of literature is important because one may visualize with its help the factors that contributed to success or failure in the actual case sof nonviolent movements. Having reached that point, a scholar interested in reconstructing peaceful techniques may consider the problem of how far the factors of success may be recreated now and those of failure may be avoided. One chief method of the reconstruction of the theory and technique of peace is that of case-study and this method requires a thorough investigation of various movements covering the adoption of all important types of peaceful techniques and then evolving, on the basis of that investigation, principles of the theory and practice of peace. Recently a few commendable studies have come out on peace movements in various parts of the world.[111] Except Fenner Brockway's *Non-Cooperation in Other Lands* [112], all other books on the history of nonviolent movements written in earlier times were purely of the nature of a historical narrative.

In his *Nonviolent Action: How It Works*[113], George Lakey discusses three mechanisms of nonviolent action—coercion, conversion, and persuasion. *Creative Conflict in Politics*[114] by Gene Sharp examines critically traditional answers to the problem of political conflict and suggests how a newly constructed technique can be used in the resolution of various types of political conflicts. Two other publications dealing with the tactics of nonviolent action are *Unarmed Strategy: Notes on Research and Analysis of Nonviolent Struggles*[115] by Johan Galtung and Gene Sharp and *A Manual for Direct Action: Strategy and Tactics for Civil Rights and all Other*

[111] For a detailed bibliography on the history of nonviolent movements see April Carter, David Hoggett, and Adam Roberts, *Nonviolent Action—Theory and Practice: A Selected Bibliography* (London, 1966) pp. 19-37.

[112] Fenner A. Brockway, *Non-Cooperation in Other Lands* (Madras, 1921).

[113] George Lakey, *Nonviolent Action: How It Works* (Wallingford, Pennsylvania, 1963).

[114] Gene Sharp, *Creative Conflict in Politics* (London, 1962).

[115] Johan Galtung and Gene Sharp, *Unarmed Strategy: Notes on Research and Analysis of Nonviolent Struggles* (Hyderabad, 1958).

Protest Movements[116] by Martin Oppenheimer and George Lakey.

The latest and current phase of nonviolent resistance to evil and injustice is represented by the Negroes' fight against racial discrimination. Quite a few useful studies have been published on this phase and they bring out the significance of various new dimensions of techniques of peaceful resistance. One among such studies is *Stride Towards Freedom*[117] by Martin Luther King. The author narrates the story of the famous struggle of 1955-56 in Montgomery against the insulting treatment of Negroes on buses. But the book offers something more than a mere story. It tells us that the theory and technique of peaceful resistance have to be modified in each individual case. King gives in his book a broad outline along which modification might proceed. The problem of technique is also taken up by Edward Clayton in his *The Negro Politician*.[118] Clayton starts with the assumption that with Negro Americans becoming politically aware, the United States is facing a crisis. He deals with the role of Negro politicians in the total scheme of political affairs and then examines what that role has meant in local and national elections. Thus the book is intended to be useful to both the Negroes and others. It will help Negroes in evaluating their importance in the complexities of American politics and it will also be a source of enlightenment about the significance of the Negroes' role for the future. Clayton tells us in a very interesting style the story of how various groups and individuals within the Negro movement have been clamouring for leadership. Clayton paints an optimistic future and asserts that the Negroes have an effective type of leadership, both actual and potential. Besides devoting quite some space to the leadership qualities and successes of Martin Luther King, he also discusses some other leaders of a junior order that show promise of developing good leadership qualities in the future. If new leadership is developing among Negroes, it is a good sign, because the success of a peaceful social movement depends largely on continued effective leadership.

---

[116] Martin Oppenheimer and George Lakey, *A Manual for Direct Action: Strategy and Tactics for Civil Rights and all Other Protest Movements* (Chicago, 1965).
[117] Martin Luther King, *Stride Towards Freedom* (London, 1959).
[118] Edward T. Clayton, *The Negro Politician* (Chicago, 1964).

It has often been seen that social movements failed or achieved only partial success because good leaders passed away before the fulfilment of the movement. However, one thing is clear from Clayton's book and that is that Negroes are no longer interested in the mere achievement of certain rights and privileges on the basis of equality with the White but also in participating in the American political process in general.

But the collapse of colour prejudice is a two-way traffic. Colour prejudice collapses not only out of a desire for collapse on the part of those who have been the sufferers but also out of a readiness to accept such a collapse by those who have been responsible for the sufferings. The struggle of the Negroes has been going on since 1890, but it was the late President Kennedy, the first US President after Abraham Lincoln to do so, who declared publicly that racial segregation and discrimination are morally indefensible. He was also the first President to support the Negroes' drive for equality by making a public announcement that the security of a nation and its future and honour depended upon the guarantee of civil rights to all citizens on an equal footing. He provided the second condition for the collapse of the frontiers of colour prejudice. It is not surprising, therefore, that Harry Golden should have thought of *Mr. Kennedy and the Negroes*[119] as a title for his book which he considers a befitting tribute to the memory of the "Second Emancipator President". Broadly speaking, this book makes a serious analysis of the entire Negro movement and a deep study of the late President Kennedy's total commitment to that social revolution. It also pinpoints the remarkable victory which the Kennedy Administration was able to achieve in preparing the way for the collapse of race prejudice within as short a span as two years and ten months. His conclusion is that if everything recommended by the late President Kennedy were granted to Negroes, the problem of colour would be solved in no time.

On the other hand, Lewis Killian and Charles Grigg, the authors of *Racial Crisis in America: Leadership in Conflict,*[120] adopt a "conflict model". They hold that the story of the struggle

---

[119] Harry Golden, *Mr. Kennedy and the Negroes* (New York, 1964).
[120] Lewis Killian and Charles Grigg, *Racial Crisis in America: Leadership in Conflict* (Englewood Cliffs, 1964).

between the Negroes and segregationists tells us that a major racial conflict in the United States is yet to occur. They take a generally pessimistic view of the progress made thus far. According to them, whatever is claimed to be an achievement in the direction of the collapse of race prejudice has been only at a very superficial level. So much so that the problems arising from the economic and cultural deprivation of the mass of Negroes still continue and, in the authors' view, they could be solved only if fundamental changes are brought about in American society. Unfortunately the character of those fundamental changes is nowhere clearly stated. In any case, the conflict model provided by Killian and Grigg has some relevance because a complete racial conciliation or harmony is possible only when there is a consensus. This consensus, as sociology teaches us, comes through various stages. In the case of the Whites and the Negroes, the present phase of confrontation between them should be concerned with the Whites learning to respect the Negroes before they can accept them as friends and equals. In other words, the success of the Negro movement should be measured in terms of its ability to persuade the White to accept the new *status quo*. But this acceptance should be based on a moral justification of the change, which in turn should be inspired by equalitarian values. However, the inadequacy of the two authors lies in their total emphasis on the conflict part of the White-Negro confrontation to the neglect of the cocperation part. A balanced view is required in a study of any subject and that is what this book by Killian and Grigg lacks.

There are two special issues of quarterly periodicals devoted to the Negro movement. These two issues are on "The Negro American"[121] and "The Negro Protest"[122] and cover all possible aspects of the subject.

NONVIOLENT CIVIL DEFENCE

An important aspect of the evolution of peaceful inter-

[121] "The Negro American", *Daedalus* (Cambridge, Mass.), Fall 1965, pp. 743-1173; "The Negro American-2", *Ibid.*, Winter 1966, pp. 1-454.

[122] "The Negro Protest", *Annals of the American Academy of Political and Social Science,* Vol. 357, January 1965, pp. 1-126.

national relations is the problem of how to deal with aggression by nonviolent means. This problem is the problem of civil defence. The concept of civil defence is not new and it has its significance even in a traditional war fought with physical force on both sides. But peace research has given an entirely new meaning to the concept of "civil defence" or "civilian defence" by using these terms to refer to defence by nonviolent means. The world has had experience of sporadic cases of nonviolent response to aggression and tyranny by means of boycott, passive resistance, strike, and non-cooperation. Peace research proceeds with the assumption that so long as a perfectly peaceable international society is not established, aggression is likely to take place and such an aggression should be met nonviolently. It also assumes that a systematic and comprehensive strategy of nonviolent defence can be built up on the basis of past experiences in nonviolent responses. Therefore, nonviolent civil defence is a problem with which peace research is closely connected. In its totality, the problem of nonviolent civil defence is the problem of finding out an alternative to war. A complete strategy of nonviolent civil defence is yet to develop. But quite a few attempts have recently been made in that direction. The attempt which deserves first mention is "The Political Equivalent of War—Civilian Defense"[123] by Gene Sharp. This study starts with the assumption that historically war has served a number of functions, the most important of which being that it has provided the ultimate sanction of international relations. What is needed, according to Sharp, is a substitute which could replace war as a means of defending freedom and as a way of life against tyranny and aggression. This substitute has to be capable of providing the necessary protection without military armaments. A non-military policy to deter attack and defend freedom would be the "political equivalent of war". Sharp believes that the way to peace lies in the adoption of this political equivalent. Thus what the world needs today is not so much disarmament as "transarmament"; a term which refers to a complete change from a military defence system to a nonviolent defence system.[124]

[123] Gene Sharp, "The Political Equivalent of War—Civilian Defense", *International Conciliation* (New York), No. 555, November 1965, pp. 5-67.
[124] The term "transarmament" was coined by Theodor Ebert.

This is what Sharp calls a "third approach". Having discussed the relevance of the third approach, Sharp proceeds to deal with the nature of a civilian defence policy and the questions he examines in that context are: How can a civilian defence policy work as a deterrent? How should preparations be made for nonviolent defence? What should be the strategy of a people defending themselves nonviolently? Sharp answers these and the like questions in the light of his understanding of the current problem of peace and suggests certain specific policy formulations with the help of his study of some recent cases of nonviolent responses. Thus Sharp's monograph on the subject is indeed interesting.[125]

Equally interesting is a paper on "Nonmilitary Defence"[126] by Arne Naess. It also discusses the problem of how an effective alternative to military defence can be found out. Suggesting nonviolent defence as the alternative, Arne Naess stipulates a scheme by which the alternative could be made effective. What discipline should a people offering nonviolent defence undergo? What course should be adopted at the time of aggression? What should nonviolent defenders do in case their country has been occupied by an aggressor? All these and the related questions have been dealt with by Arne Naess in a scientific and convincing manner. The scheme that he suggests is the result of a careful analysis of some cases of the use of nonviolence in world history and its implementation in modern conditions. The scheme may not be a blueprint to be applied anywhere and everywhere, and the author does not make any such claim either, but it certainly indicates a direction for the construction of a better and more effective technique of nonviolence, and to that extent Arne Naess has made a valuable contribution.

There are two other important studies on civilian defence. One is *Civilian Defence*,[127] a collection of essays by Adam Roberts, Jerome Frank, Arne Naess, and Gene Sharp; and the

---

[125] A fuller study of the subject would soon be available in Gene Sharp's forthcoming book on *The Politics of Nonviolent Action*.

[126] Arne Naess, "Nonmilitary Defence", in Quincy Wright, William M. Evan, and Morton Deutsch, eds., *Preventing World War III*, pp. 123-35.

[127] Adam Roberts, Jerome Frank, Arne Naess, and Gene Sharp, *Civilian Defence* (London, 1964).

other is a special issue of the periodical *Pax*.[128] The contributions made by the four eminent scholars to *Civilian Defence* are "A Case for Civilian Defence", "Psychological Problems in the Elimination of War", "Non-Military Defence and Foreign Policy", and "Deterrence and Liberation by Civilian Defence". It is learnt that a booklet of a somewhat similar nature, but incorporating the problems of India's nonviolent defence, will soon be brought out by the Gandhi Peace Foundation.

The special issue of *Pax* devoted to the problem of nonviolent defence contains articles on all possible aspects. In his article, "Towards a New Concept of Defence", Johan Galtung maintains that the question what to defend is more important than the question how to defend. He makes a distinction between social defence and territorial defence. Military defence is a territorial type; and guerrilla warfare and nonviolent defence are social types. There are ten important aspects of guerrilla warfare—geographical requirements, democratic ideology, involvement of a majority of the population, the strategic doctrine of attacking where the opponent is weak rather than head-on, the exchange relationship between the civilian population and the guerrillas, relation with the enemy, ideologization of conflict, sabotage, logistics and support, and defence against guerrillas. In most of these aspects a striking similarity with nonviolent defence is found. Galtung suggests that in view of the remarkable successes of post-war guerrilla campaigns and the large number of reports on them, the guerrilla campaigns should be studied for obtaining experience that could be useful in planning a nonviolent social defence. Lars Parsholt, maintains in his paper, "Civilian Resistance to Occupation", the importance of the distinction between general and organized resistance. The former would include a general norm against offering services to the occupying power. Parsholt holds that services which would help in the production of nuclear weapons should not be performed even in the case of requisitions. This may be contrary to the Hague Convention but, if so, international law itself should be changed. Resistance should be firm in order to be effective. Other rules for general resistance are the refusal to assist in disseminating propaganda and to help

[128] *Pax* (Oslo), February 1965, pp. 1-32.

the administration. Another paper included in *Pax* is "Training for Nonviolent Defence" by Theodor Oslon who believes that training for nonviolent civilian defence can be discussed programmatically under four heads: (a) when advocates are building leadership cadres and acting with these groups on pressing social problems; (b) when making direct approaches to government, with training and experimentation, both co-operative and competitive, with government's armed forces; (c) when training is done with the resources of government; and (d) during the period of refining, retraining, refreshing, and extension of training to the whole populace. He asserts that we should stress specific orientation to maintaining our way of life rather than emphasizing technical and conspiratorial skills. Torstein Dale holds in his "Nonviolence as Seen from a Military Point of View" that trench warfare between pacifists and adherents of military defence is slowly coming to an end and that increasing emphasis is being put now on the peace-keeping functions of the defence establishment and at the same time pacifists are moving from a negative to a constructive position. The maintenance of peace calls for a well prepared system of combined nonviolent and military efforts in national defence and for international peace-keeping forces. Therefore, Dale makes a powerful plea that both military and nonviolent means must be studied non-dogmatically. Gunnar Garbo maintains in his "A New Dialogue" that the solutions which were valid in the thirties are no more tenable, because thet hreat of a nuclear holocaust has made war suicidal. In this situation, occupation may be a choice preferable to war. We must, therefore, evaluate the significance of civilian resistance for the defence capacity of democracies and this could best be done by arranging a dialogue between pacifists and proponents of military defence. Johanne Reutz Gjermoe emphasizes on the other hand, in his paper entitled, "Why Civilian Defence?", that nonviolent civilian defence cannot be applied simultaneously with acts of violence and sabotage and that it has a better chance of success during military occupation. Nonviolent civilian defence is not solely a method or a technique but a principle on which we must build a new cooperative social order. "Nonviolent Defence and Peace Policy" by Lars Parsholt tells us how nonviolence can be made the basis of a country's foreign policy. Nonviolence can be effective in preventing ideological-political control and also to some extent in preventing the exploitation of the country for resources or as a nuclear base. Nonviolence is a better peace policy because it avoids nuclear provocation. Norway, by shifting the emphasis towards nonviolence and by renouncing all thoughts of participation in western nuclear strategy, can help overcome the vicious circle of mutual suspicion. There is yet another article in *Pax,* Nils Petter Gleditsch's "Nonviolent Defence as a Strategic Different".

According to Gleditsch, a serious problem about nonviolent defence is how to make the nonviolent deterrent credible. Commitment to resistance and communication of the strength as well as of commitment are among the major factors in the credibility. Commitment to sabotage of one's own airfields and communications could conceivably be an automatic technical arrangement, but greater stress should be laid on the human commitment. The author is of the view that the impression that nonviolent defence strengthens the nuclear deterrence is false. Thus the papers included in the special issue of *Pax* cover quite a wide field of the problem of civil defence. The papers, however, are all written in the Norwegian language and a person like the present surveyor has to depend on the English summary given at the end of each paper. Perhaps these papers can be of greater value and reach a larger readership if they are translated into English in full.

A mention should be made here of a series of three articles by Theodor Ebert. Published under the general title of civil defence, they deal with "Risks Facing an Invader",[129] "Sabotage and Guerrilla Tactics",[130] and "Effects of Repression by the Invader".[131] In the first article the author maintains that the success of a nonviolent civilian defence against an invader lies in the resister's capacity to change the intentions of the aggressor and to liberate the opponent from the evils of his own system. In the second article he lays down another condition of the

---

[129] Theodor Ebert, "Risks Facing an Invader", *Peace News*, No. 1498, 12 March 1965, p. 6.
[130] Theodor Ebert, "Sabotage and Guerrilla Warfare", *Ibid.*, p. 7.
[131] Theodor Ebert, "Effects of Repression", *Ibid.*, No. 1499, 19 March 1965, pp. 10, 11.

success of a nonviolent civilian defence. This condition is the avoidance of a combination of the terror methods of guerrilla warfare and nonviolent resistance. Terrorist activities, though they may be inspired by pure patriotism, reduce the effectiveness of nonviolent resistance, because the aggressor regards nonviolence as a camouflage for the preparation of a great terrorist plot. Therefore, Ebert suggests that two precautions must be taken in a nonviolent defence. One is the wide dissemination of a warning, before the aggression occurs and the nonviolent resistance starts, demolishing mistaken ideas about terrorist patriotism and showing the disadvantages of such patriotism to the ultimate success of nonviolent resistance; and the other is that the resisters must be prepared to protect the lives of invaders if and when terrorist activities occur in spite of the warning. In the third article, Ebert underlines a tactical principle of nonviolent resistance, that is, to force the opponent to pause for reflection.

The problem of nonviolent civil defence is closely related to the question of nonviolent resistance as a national defence policy. This question has been taken up in recent years by quite a few authors. Bradford Lyttle, for example, discusses this question in his *National Defence Thru Nonviolent Resistance*.[132] Other publications on this question are *Speak Truth to Power*,[133] *Alternative to War*[134] by R.G. Bell, *Unilateral Initiatives and Disarmament*[135] by Mulford Sibley, *An Alternative to War*[136] by Gordon Zahn, and *Peacemakers: A World Reborn*.[137]

Even if nonviolent resistance is adopted as a national defence policy, it involves the problem of strategy and of the role of the individual. The first problem is dealt with by Joan Bondurant in her *Paraguerilla Strategy: A New Concept in Arms Control*[138] and by the contributors to *Pathogenesis of*

---

[132] Bradford Lyttle, *National Defence Thru Nonviolent Resistance* (Chicago, 1958).
[133] American Friends Service Committee, *Speak Truth to Power* (Philadelphia, 1955).
[134] R.G. Bell, *Alternative to War* (London, 1959).
[135] Mulford Q. Sibley, *Unilateral Initiatives and Disarmament* (Philadelphia, 1962).
[136] Gordon Zahn, *An Alternative to War* (New York, 1963).
[137] *Peacemakers: A World Reborn* (London, 1963).
[138] Joan V. Bondurant, *Paraguerilla Strategy: A New Concept in Arms Control* (Berkeley, 1963).

War[139] which has been edited by Margaret Penrose, whereas the second problem is taken care of by Ralph Templin in his *Democracy and Nonviolence: The Role of the Individual in World Crisis*.[140] Templin is led to the conclusion that the practice of nonviolence so far has not contributed to the development of positive techniques of influence and that, therefore, it is quite probable that violence would be used in case a nonviolent group gets arms. In the international sphere, one such possible situation can be imagined when nations achieve national independence. The same note of anxiety about the future of peaceful resistance is struck in *The Quiet Battle: Writings on the Theory and Practice of Nonviolent Resistance*,[141] edited by Mulford Sibley. The main argument of this collection of essays is that there exist elaborate techniques to impede the choice of negative actions but no effective technique to channel interaction into desired direction. Peace research has to take note of this problem.

No survey like the present one can ignore two studies published recently. One is *Toward A Strategy of Peace*[142], edited by Walter Clemens and the other is *Violence or Nonviolence*,[143] by Victor Wolfenstein. Both the books deal with the technique of peaceful resistance. The first book contains essays which examine obstacles to peace and suggest approaches to pace, whereas the second assert that personality factors are important determinants of the kinds of political means chosen by nonviolent resisters. Thus both the publications are useful for an understanding of the problems and possibilities of civil defence.

It does not require much discussion to realize how important is the problem of nonviolent civilian defence, especially in the context of today when internal war is fast replacing international war as an instrument of national policy. No efforts can bring enduring peace unless this phenomenon of internal wars is controlled. The nature of internal wars and how they

[139] Margaret Penrose, ed., *Pathogenesis of War* (London, 1963).
[140] Ralph T. Templin, *Democracy and Nonviolence: The Role of the Individual in World Crisis* (Boston, 1965).
[141] Mulford Q. Sibley, *The Quiet Battle: Writings on the Theory and Practice of Nonviolent Resistance* (New York, 1964).
[142] Walter C. Clemens, Jr., ed., *Toward A Strategy of Peace* (Chicago, 1965).
[143] E. Victor Wolfenstein, *Violence or Nonviolence* (Princeton, 1965).

can be prevented from disturbing the peace of the world are the questions to which the book entitled *Internal War*[144] is addressed. Edited by Harry Eckstein, this book explores the nature and types of "internal war" by which its contributors broadly understand attempts to achieve basic political objectives by means of violence. Contributors to this volume include Karl Deutsch, Talcott Parsons, Sidney Verba, Gabriel Almond, and Lucian Pye. In his *The Challenge of Modernization*[145], I.R. Sinai discusses the nature of the threat posed by modernization to the cause of peace. This book discusses the problem of underdevelopment and underprivilege in terms of the encounter between the western and other civilizations. The author gives an account of the wrenching transformations by which the west modernized itself and of the traditional societies which received the disrupting impact of western imperialism. He analyses the various problems that have arisen from the desire of new nations to modernize themselves along western lines and which he characterizes as the challenge of modernization. But the challenge, accorking to Sinai, is to the west itself and not to the new nations. He seems to believe that the ruling elites of new countries are nowhere capable of solving the tremendous problems before them and that all the developing countries are in the process of disintegration. He also believes that modernization in developing countries can be effected only in an authoritarian rather than in a democratic framework. This clearly presents a dismal picture of the prospects of lasting peace because any trend towards authoritarianism is bound to hamper the cause of peace ultimately. On the other hand, Kenneth Boulding has given us an extremely provocative book, *The Meaning of the Twentieth Century*.[146] He calls the present phase of history the "post-civilized phase". It is Boulding's contention that man has moved from the nomadic to the urban, agricultural, and civilized stages of life and that the present stage is that of after-civilization. Just as man underwent a change of outlook and personality as he advanced towards civilization, he should

[144] Harry Eckstein, *Internal War* (London, 1964).
[145] I.R. Sinai, *The Challenge of Modernization* (London, 1964).
[146] Kenneth E. Boulding, *The Meaning of the Twentieth Century* (New York, 1964).

now think of an outlook relevant to or demanded by the new world of technology and supranational organizations. Boulding traces the various forces which have brought the post-civilization into being — forces like the ever-increasing power of science and technology and the world-wide network of communications. He is of the view that one of the major demands of the post-civilized phase is peace. And peace requires in concrete terms peaceful ways of resolving social, political, and psychological conflicts. The problems of war and overpopulation will have to be solved if the twentieth century of post-civilization is to achieve its real meaning. Boulding does not clearly say what is the real meaning of the twentieth century. But this meaning is clearly the achievement of a world without war. There are people who believe that the fulfilment of any such meaning is impossible. But the contributors to the book, *A Warless World*,[147] edited by Arthur Larson, believe that it is not impossible, though difficult it is. The essays included in this volume cover a variety of subjects like change in a disarmed world, the question of peaceful internal change, psychological problems of warlessness and the psychology of warless man, and the spiritual effects of warlessness. Among the contributors are Arnold Toynbee, Kenneth Boulding, Margaret Mead, W.E. Hocking, Jules Moch, Louis Sohn, and James Wadsworth. Each of the eleven contributors has written in the light of his own special knowledge. But the editor has been able to bring their ideas into such a consistent whole as to present a correct appraisal of the immediate needs and problems of a disarmed world. Special mention should be made here of three papers. One is by Louis Sohn who dispels the fears of those who think that a disarmed world will be dominated by complete anarchy; the other is by Jules Moch who riducules the idea that a disarmed world will not be able to solve the problem of national security; and the third is by Arnold Toynbee who assures that human progress will not stop if peaceful methods are employed for social change. The same optimism about the possibility of a warless world runs through Walter Millis' *A World Without War*.[148] In this connexion one should also take notice of *One-Dimensional*

---

[147] Arthur Larson, ed. *A Warless World* (New York, 1963).
[148] Walter Millis, *A World Without War* (Santa Barbara, 1961).

Man[149] by Herbert Marcuse. The problem to which Marcuse addresses himself is how to reconcile originality and spontaneity and all the human creativity with the prevailing drive towards rationality which wants to reduce everything to one universal system of thought and action. He makes it clear that the choice before mankind is between extinction and survival. According to him, atomic war is not only a threat to human survival but is giving greater and greater incentives to the advancement of industrial society. This industrial society is irrational as a whole, because its productivity is destructive of the free development of the individual and because its peace is maintained only with a constant threat of war.

This survey is by no means exhaustive. It includes only those items which this writer considers important among the ones available in this country. Since peace research is yet a neglected field in India, even the best libraries do not have sufficient material on the subject. If peace research programme develops in India, the aquisition of relevant literature would be the first requirement. In any case, this bibliographical survey would give, it is hoped, a fairly broad introdution to the reader about the range of peace research that is being done in other countries. It may also indicate gaps that may be filled up by peace research in India either in the national context or in the international context.

[149] Herbert Marcuse, *One-Dimensional Man* (London, 1964).

Appendices and Index

APPENDICES

This section of the monograph on "Current Peace Research and India" is in the nature of an inventory of various centres of peace research in the world. The information collected here is by no means exhaustive, except in the sense that whatever data are available in India have been sorted and classified in as systematic a way as possible. It is not claimed, therefore, that the following appendices would give us a complete introduction of the various centres of peace research and their activities. The various centres selected here, however, have been divided into two categories: those working directly in the field of peace research; and those which have a part of their research programme devoted to peace research. The institutions belonging to the first category have been covered in Appendix A with a brief introduction about them, whereas those belonging to the second category have only been listed in Appendix B. Besides giving a list of centres of peace research, this section also gives a list each of the important periodicals in the field of peace research and of those conference, which are held regularly at definite intervals. These periodicals and conferences have been given in Appendix C and Appendix D respectively.

APPENDIX A

CANADIAN PEACE RESEARCH INSTITUTE, Box 70, Clarkson, Ontario, Canada.

Established in 1961, the Canadian Peace Research Institute (CPRI) has been doing commendable work in the field of peace research under the directorship of Norman Alcock. From its very inception, it has given attention to the problem of informing and educating people about the importance of research on problems of peace. In order to contribute to the achievement of this objective, the Institute has so far undertaken a number of research projects which deal mainly with disarmament and its impact on world peace. An important study planned by the CPRI is "The Theory of Social Change with Particular Emphasis on the Institution of War".

The greater contribution of the Institute, however, is in the field of reference service. It publishes a monthly *Information Report* on research in progress (obtainable from 341, Bloor St., West, Toronto, Canada). *Peace Research Abstracts* (25, Dundana Avenue, Dundas, Ontario, Canada) is another useful publication of the Institute. Edited by Alan Newcombe and Hanna Newcombe, this journal contains abstracts of articles on war and peace published in various periodicals. Its goal is complete coverage of the literature in all languages from 1945 to the present. Although this goal is still far from realization, the scope of the *Peace Research Abstracts* has been gradually expanding. So much so that each monthly issue now contains about 750 abstracts of papers in English, Norwegian, Danish, Dutch, German, Russian, Polish, and Czech. In addition, a new series of monographs has been started under the title "Peace Research Reviews" from 1966. This series has been conceived of as an answer to the need for concise and readable literature. Bi-monthly booklets will also be published under this series. Three subjects on which booklets are also soon are "History of Disarmament Negotiations"; "Revolutions and Civil Strife"; and "Non-violence: Strategy or Technique".

Besides the publication programme, the CPRI has also been organizing international seminars on peace, either by its ownself or in collaboration with bodies like Institute for International Order, New York.

INSTITUTE FOR PEACE AND CONFLICT RESEARCH, Dronningensgade 14 II, Copenhagen K, Denmark.

This Institute was established in December 1964. It has a small full-time staff as well as several part-timers. The research programme of the IPCR is being developed. The activities launched by the Institute so far have been mainly in collaboration with the Peace Research Institute, Oslo; and Peace Research Centre, Lancaster. In February 1966, the IPCR organized the Second Nordic Conference on Peace Research.

DANISH CONFLICT RESEARCH GROUP, Schimmelmannsrej 31, Denmark.

This Group was organized in April 1964. Its main activity consists in participation in seminars organized either by itself or by institutions in Scandinavian countries. It has established a number of working groups to study the contribution of social sciences to conflict resolution. These working groups are in the fields of international politics and political science, psychology, sociology, economics, and philosophy. They are working on subjects that centre around interdisciplinary problems. The objective behind the establishment of these working groups is to prepare an interdisciplinary synthesis of topics relating to the study of conflict. Since September 1964 the Danish Conflict Research Group has also been publishing a newsletter giving an account of peace research activities in all the Nordic countries. Besides, the Group also has a plan to arrange for the circulation of research monographs by its members in mimeographed form.

HARRY S. TRUMAN CENTRE FOR THE ADVANCEMENT OF PEACE,
Hebrew University of Jerusalem, Jerusalem, Israel.

This newly established Centre will be a part of the Hebrew University of Jerusalem. It will devote its research efforts mainly to the application of scientific methods to the identification and removal of the causes of war. But it will also undertake studies in international law, comparative religion, Asian and African studies, and political theory. Special projects would be related to Israel's experience in social and cultural integration of plural communities. Beside the Asian and African libraries of the Hebrew University, the Centre will house the Martin Buber Library, the official United Nations Library in Israel, and parts of Albert Einstein's personal library. It is also reported that the Centre will award an annual Peace Prize of 50,000 dollars.

HESBJERG COLLEGE, Pr., Holmstrup, Fyn, Denmark.

Since 1964, the Hesbjerg College has been holding an international summer school on the theme of peace and research. The lectures are delivered by resident tutors and visiting scholars from British and Scandinavian universities representing the major social science disciplines. A large variety of subjects have so far been covered in these lectures. They include peace research and the resolution of conflict, nature of peace research, the nature of a peaceful society, history of peace movements, and the socio-psychological factors of war and peace.

THE INTERNATIONAL PEACE RESEARCH INSTITUTE, P. O. Box 5052, Oslo, Norway.

Formerly the Section for Research on Conflict and Peace of the Institute for Social Research, Oslo, the International Peace Research Institute was established as an independent body in January 1966 with Johan Galtung as its Director. During the transformation period, the Institute was known as Peace Research Institute, Oslo (PRIO). Thus what was only a national institute became international in character. Eversince its internationalization, the Institute has been intensifying its research activity by arranging peace research conferences, inviting scholars from different parts of the world, and bringing out publications on various subjects. The subjects on which special lecture series have been organized include peace theory, international relations theory, and methodology of peace research. The Institute also publishes a quarterly journal called *Journal of Peace Research*. Besides, there is also a series of monographs meant for the publication of research findings beyond the article format. More than twenty-five research monographs have already been published. In addition, a series of pamphlets in Norwegian is also published. A detailed programme of research to be undertaken in the near future has been announced.

INTERNATIONAL PEACE AND CONFLICT RESEARCH INSTITUTE, Stockholm, Sweden.

Established on 1 July 1966, this Institute is also known as the Stockholm International Peace Research Institute (SIPRI). It has been founded by the

Government of Sweden. This fact is of great significance. For it shows that peace research is becoming respectable even among governments. The SIPRI is to be international in its scope of studies, in its research staff, and in its governance.

THE ATLANTIC INSTITUTE, 24 Quai du 4-Septembe, Boulogne-sur-Siene, France.

This Institute publishes a Clearing House Bulletin of current and prospective studies in the Atlantic field undertaken by institutions in Western Europe and North America. This bulletin is called *Atlantic Studies*. Its scope covers studies that have a focus on relations and coordination of policies of the Atlantic countries.

THE FRENCH INSTITUTE OF POLEMOLOGY, 15 avenue du President - Wilson, Paris XVI, France.

The Institute has published several books dealing with the sociology of war and peace in French. They have been translated into several languages including English. The Institute brings out a quarterly journal called *War and Peace* containing original articles on the psychology of individual and collective aggressiveness and analysis of past and present conflicts. Besides, abstracts of French and foreign works connected with polemology are also covered in this journal.

THE ATHENIAN INSTITUTE OF ANTHROPOS, 8 Dem. Soutsou St., Athens 602, Greece.

The Institute developed as a result of the desire of a group of behavioural scientists in the early fifties to have an interdisciplinary research and training centre. In its present form, it was organized in 1962. It puts great emphasis on international collaboration in research. It publishes a mimeographed newsletter in English.

RESEARCH CENTRE ON SOCIAL AND ECONOMIC DEVELOPMENT IN SOUTHERN ASIA, University Enclave, Delhi, India.

The research activities of this Centre cover sociology, social psychology, political science, economics, and demography. The Centre has recently published an up-to-date *Southern Asia Social Science Bibliography*. It also publishes a *Current Research Information Bulletin*.

ISRAELI INSTITUTE OF INTERNATIONAL AFFAIRS, Tel Aviv, POB 17027, Israel.

This Institute has created a working group which functions as a branch of the International Peace Research Association of the Netherlands. The group has so far organized various discussions on peace research and on peaceful solution of the Arab-Israel conflict. The findings of the members of the group are published (in Hebrew and French) in the quarterly journal *International Problems*.

THE POLEMOLOGICAL INSTITUTE, University of Groningen, Ubbo Emmiussingel 19, Groningen, Netherlands.

This Institute was established at the Groningen State University in 1961 as an independent body under the faculty of law, with a view to studying the factors leading to war and the conditions under which peae and a system of international law may be maintained. Since its establishment, the Institute has made several studies, both independently and in collaboration with other institutions, of problems relating to war and peace, though these studies have been published in the Dutch language. Recently, the Institute also initiated a new series of publications in the field of war and peace problems. This series is called "Attitudes in World Problems". Besides, the Institute also gives a course in peace research for all students interested in the subject. The Institute also publishes a *Newsletter*.

THE CONFLICT RESEARCH SOCIETY, Faculty of Laws, University College, Gower St., London, W.C. 1.

This Society is mainly concerned with providing facilities for an exchange of views between the supporters of different approaches to conflict resolution.

THE UNITED WORLD TRUST, 29 Great James St., London, W.C. I.

This Trust works for peace by arranging conferences and seminars and by encouraging research. It organized the "Civilian Defence Study Conference" in September 1964 and is now planning a long-term research programme on nonviolence.

THE INSTITUTE FOR POLICY STUDIES, 1900 Florida Ave., N.W. Washington D.C. 20009, U.S.A.

It is an independent centre of research, education, and social invention on problems of public policy. The publications of the Institute are in the field of foreign policy, development of new political structures, and education policy.

THE CARNEGIE ENDOWMENT FOR INTERNATIONAL PEACE, 345 E., 46th St., New York, U.S.A.

Established more than fifty years ago, the Endowment has been doing commendable work for the promotion of the cause of peace. Besides holding conferences on various aspects of peace, the Endowment has brought out a large number of publications and it also publishes, five times in a year, a journal called *International Conciliation*.

CENTRE FOR RESEARCH ON CONFLICT RESOLUTION, University of Michigan, Ann Arbor, Michigan, U.S.A.

This Centre is one of the most important institutions engaged in the study of conflict and its resolution. A number of research monographs have been brought out by the centre. The Centre has a fellowship programme for the study of conflict resolution. Frequent seminars on peace research are also arranged. The quarterly journal of the Centre, *Journal of Conflict Resolution,* publishes valuable articles in the field of conflict studies.

THE LANCASTER PEACE RESEARCH CENTRE, 71, Church St., Lancaster, U.K.

The Lancaster Peace Research Centre is in charge of the conflict studies programme at the University of Lancaster. From the March 1966 issue of the Centre's *Newsletter* it appears that the Centre has a very imaginative research design for case studies of conflict. A number of the staff members of the Centre contributed papers to the Second Nordic Peace Research Conference held at Copenhagen in 1966. The Centre has been cooperating with the Hesbjerg College in Denmark and various other institutions in the study of peace research.

THE INSTITUTE FOR TRAINING IN NONVIOLENCE, Hendon Ave., Finchley, London N. 3, U.K.

This Institute was established with the assumption that those who are involved in peace work and nonviolent social action need training. By "action" is meant the ability to work spontaneously and transform the human situation for the better. The Institute, therefore, aims at building a nonviolent movement which is guided by a vision of a new social order. Such a movement obviously requires people who can take upon themselves the burden of acting as "change-agents" to bring about a new order. The Institute aseeks to help this process by providing a centre where we can learn from each other's experience ways of developing a nonviolent movement.

One of the important activities of the Institute, therefore, is to organize monthly seminars. Chief among the subjects on which the Institute has already held seminars include "Action Research and Training in Nonviolence","Meaning of Christian Action for Peace and Social Change", and "The Conscientious Objector and Training for a Peace Brigade". The Institute also has a lecture series, called the *Gandhi Memorial Lecture Series*.

The Institute has a publication programme also. It has already published several small booklets which include "Action Research and Training for Nonviolence" and "Towards a Nonviolent Social Order". The choice of subjects for research, however, is left to the researcher. For the Institute has the belief that respect for self-chosen task is an essential of the relationship based on nonviolence.

The Institute aims at developing into a residential centre eventually.

APPENDIX B

Institute of Philosophy and Sociology, 72 rue Nowy Swait, Warsaw, Poland.

The Ciba Foundation, 41 Portland Place, London, U.K.

The Institute of World Economy and International Relations, Moscow, U.S.S.R.

Centre for the Study of Democratic Institutions, Santa Barbara, California, U.S.A.

School of International Affairs, Columbia University, New York, U.S.A.

The Institute for Social Research, New York, U.S.A.

Peace Research and Education Project, 1100 E. Washington St., Ann Arbor, Michigan, U.S.A.

Rockey Mountains — Great Plains Peace Research, Colorado State University, Fort Collins, Colorado, U.S.A.

Studies in International Conflict and Integration, Stanford University, Stanford, California, U.S.A.

The Society for the Psychological Study of Social Issues, P.O. Box 1248, Ann Arbor, Michigan, U.S.A.

The Social Science Research Council, 230 Park Ave., N.Y. 10017, U.S.A.

The World Law Fund, 11 W. 42nd St., N.Y. 10036, U.S.A.

The Council for the Study of Mankind, P.O. Box Santa Monica, California, U.S.A.

The Institute for International Order, 11 W. 42nd St., N.Y. 10036, U.S.A.

The International Confederation for Disarmament and Peace, The Grange, 3 Hendon Ave., London N. 3, U.K.

The International Commission of Jurists, 2 quai du Cheval-Blance, Geneva, Switzerland.

The International Peace Bureau, 41 rue de Zurich, Geneva, Switzerland.

The World Academy of Arts and Sciences, 1 Ruppin St. Rehovot, P.O. Box 534, Israel.

The World Federation of Scientific Workers, 40 Goodge St. London, W. 1, U.K.

The World Peace Through World Law Centre, 400 Hill Building, Washington D.C., U.S.A.

The Association of German Scientists, Bonn 53, West Germany.

The Japan Society for the Promotion of Science, Tokyo, Japan.

The Hague Academy of International Law, The Hague, Netherlands.

The Swedish Foreign Policy Association, Stockholm, Norway.

The Swedish Institute of International Affairs, Stockholm, Norway.

King's College, London University, London, U.K.

The Institute for Policy Studies, 1900 Florida Ave., NW Washington D.C., U.S.A.

Cornell University Centre for International Studies, Cornell University, U.S.A.

The American Society of International Law, 2223 Massachusetts Ave., N.W. Washington, D.C., 4 St., U.S.A.

The American Friends Service Committee 160 N. Fifteenth St., Philadelphia, U.S.A.

The Council for a Livable World, 1346 Connecticut Ave., N.W. Washington D.C., U.S.A.

Scientists on Survival, P.O. Box 334, Times Square Station, New York, U.S.A.

The Society for the Social Responsibility in Science, Gambier, Ohio, U.S.A.

The New York Peace Information Centre, 218 E. 18th St., New York, U.S.A.

National Committee for a Sane Nuclear Policy, 17 East 45th St., New York, U.S.A.

The Upland Institute, Upland Ave., Chester, Pennsylvania, U.S.A.

The World Federation of Scientific Workers, 40 Goodge St., London, W 1, U.K.

The Royal Institute of International Affairs, Av. de la couronne, 88, Brussels 5, Belgium.

The Association for International Cooperation and Disarmament, Box 247, P.O. Haymarket, N.S.W., Australia.

The Seletun Foundation for Development Research and Consultation, Christies Gate 16, Bergen, Norway

The Swedish Folk University, University of Uppsala, Sweden.

The Economic Commission of the Soviet Peace Committee, U.S.S.R.

The Brookings Institution, 1775 Massachusets Ave., N.W., Washington D.C., U.S.A.

The University of Chicago Centre for Human Understanding, 2726 N S5., N.W. Washington D.C., U.S.A.

Institute for the Study of Violence, Brandeis University, Walthan, Mass., U.S.A.

Hudson Institute, Quaker Ridge Road, Harmon-on-Hudson, New York, U.S.A.

The Conference on Peace Research in History, 1900 Florida Ave., N.W. Washington D.C., U.S.A.

The International Union of Peace Societies, 1, rue J. Lefebvre, Paris 9, France.

Mankind 2000, 3 Hendon Ave., London N. 3, U.K.

Universities and the Quest for Peace, 1400 Harmann Drive, Houston, Texas, U.S.A.

The International Institute for Peace, Mollwaldplatz 5, Vienna IV, Austria.

The War Resisters' International, 88 Park Ave., Enfield, Middlesex, U.K.

The World Veterans Federation, 16 rue Hamelin, Paris 16, France.

The Peace Research Society — International, Wharton School, University of Pennsylvania, Philadelphia, Pa., U.S.A.

The United Nations Institute for Training and Research, United Nations, New York, U.S.A.

The Social Sciences Centre, 5 Koumbari St., Kolonaki St., Kolonaki Square, Athens 138, Greece.

The Israeli Institute of International Affairs, P.O. Box 17027, Tel Aviv, Israel.

The Polish Institute of International Affairs, Warsaw, ul. Warecka 1 a, Poland.

The Creighton University Centre for Peace Research, Omaha, Nebraska, U.S.A.

The Japan Peace Research and Disarmament Study Group, C/o International House of Japan, 2 Toriza ka machi, Azabu, Minato-kw, Tokyo, Japan.

The Research Centre on Social and Economic Development in Southern Asia, University Enclave, Delhi.

Campaign for Nuclear Disarmament, 2 Carthusian Street, London, E.C. 1, U.K.

International Fellowship of Reconciliation, Box 271, Newarck, New York, U.S.A.

Turn Toward Peace, Cooper Station, Box 401, New York-3, N.Y., U.S.A.

Peacemaker Training Programme, C/o Karl Meyer, 164 West Oak St., Chicago 10, Illionis, U.S.A.

Council for Correspondence, Post office Box 536, Cooper Station, New York 3, N.Y. U.S.A.

Yugoslav League for Peace, Independence and Equality of Peoples, Belgrade, Yugoslavia.

Gandhi Peace Foundation, Rajghat, New Delhi, India.

Civil Service International, Curzon Road, New Delhi, India.

Gandhian Institute of Studies, Rajghat, Varanasi, India.

APPENDIX C

War and Peace, quarterly review of the Institute of Polemology, 15, avenue du President-Wilson, Paris, XVI, France.

International Problems, quarterly journal of the Israeli Institute of International Affairs, POB 17027, Tel Aviv, Israel.

Cooperation and Conflict, semi-annual publication of Nordic Studies in International Politics, BOX 23015, Stockholm, Sweden.

International Conciliation, published five times in a year by the Carnegie Endowment for International Peace, New York, U.S.A.

Background, quarterly journal of the International Studies Association, University of Southern California, Los Angeles, California, 90007, U.S.A.

Coexistence, a semi-annual of the Pergamon Press, London.

Current Thought on Peace and War, published by the International Data and Information Center of the Wisconsin State University, Oshkosh, Wisconsin, U.S.A.

Information Bulletin on Disarmament, published by the World Veterans Federation, Paris, France.

Impact of Science on Society, published by the UNESCO, Paris France.

Journal of Conflict Resolution, quarterly journal of the Centre for Research on Conflict Resolution, Michigan University, Ann Arbor, U.S.A.

Bulletin of the Atomic Scientists, published ten times in a year by the Educational Foundation for Nuclear Science, 935 E. 60th St., Chicago, Illinois, 60637, U.S.A.

War/Peace Report, published from 8 E. 36th St., New York, N.Y. 10016, U.S.A.

War Resistance, quarterly journal of the War Resisters' Internation, Lansbury House, 88 park Ave., Enfield, Middlesex, U.K.

International Social Science Journal, quarterly journal published by the Unesco, Paris, France.

International Peace Research Newsletter, published quarterly from the Hague for the International Peace Research Association.

Our Generation Against Nuclear War, published quarterly by the Combined Universities Campaign for Nuclear Disarmament (Canada), and the Campaign for Nuclear Disarmament (U.K.)

Gandhi Marg, quarterly journal of the Gandhi Smarak Nidhi, Rajghat, New Delhi, India.

Dissent, quarterly journal published from 509 Fifth Ave., New York, N.Y. 10017, U.S.A.

Journal of Peace Research, quarterly journal of Peace Research Institute, Universitets forlaget, University of Oslo, Box 307, Blindern, Oslo 3, Norway.

   Bhoodan Yajna (Hindi)
   (Sarva Seva Sangh, Rajghat, Varanasi).

Catholic Worker
(39 Spring Street, N.Y. 12).

Confederation for Peace
(International Confederation for Disarmament and Peace, The Grange, 3 Hendon Avenue, London, N. 3).

Dissent
(509 Fifth Avenue, N.Y. 17).

Fellowship
Fellowship of Reconciliation, Box 271, Nyack, N.Y. U.S.A.

Herald of Peace
(International Peace Society, 195-7 Walworth Road, London-S.W. 1).

International Newsletter on Peace Research
(International Consultative Committee On Peace Research, 1100 E Washington Street, Ann Arbor, Michigan, U.S.A.).

Manas
Manas Publishing Co., P.O. Box, 32112, E 1 Sereno Station, Los Angeles, California, U.S.A.

New Left Review
Garliale, Street, London W.1. U.K.

New Statesman.
(Great Turnstile, London, W.C.1).

No More Hiroshimas
(Japan Council Against A & H Bombs, 7-12, Shiba Shinbashi Minato-Ku, Tokyo, Japan).

One World
National Peace Council, 29 Great James Street, London, W.C.1).

Our Generation Against Nuclear War
(Housmans, 5 Caledonian Road, London, N.1).

Peace Information Bulletin
Gandhi Peace Foundation, Rajghat, New Delhi, India.

Peace Maker
(10208 Sylvan Avenue (Gano) Cincinnati 41, Ohio).

Peace News
5 Caledonian Road, London, N. 1).

Prevent World War III.
(Society for the Prevention of World War III, 515 Madison Avenue, N.Y. 22).

Reconciliation
(9 Coombe Road, New Maldon Surrey, England).

Sane World
(17 E 45th Street, N.Y. 17).

APPENDIX D

Pugwash Conferences on Science and World Affairs, 8 Asmara Road, London, N.W. 2, U.K.

Pugwash Conferences are an attempt made mainly by scientists at discovering the scope of scientists' contribution to peace. So far sixteen such conferences have been held in different parts of the world. The last one was held at Sopot, Poland, in September 1966. A newsletter, called *Pugwash Newsletter,* is also published regularly.

European Peace Research Conference

The Peace Research Society — International (Wharton School, University of Pennsylvania, Philadelphia) has been holding a series of European Peace Research Conferences. The last one held was in Austria in September 1966. The papers presented and discussed in the Conference related to subjects like the international system, conflict and cooperation, international interdependence, and foreign policy analysis.

North American Peace Research Conferences

Organized by the University of Pennsylvania, there have been held three conferences so far under this series.

The Conference of the Universities and the Quest for Peace

INTERNATIONAL CONVOCATION ON PACEM IN TERRIS, Hilton Hotel, New York, U.S.A. ; sponsored by The Centre for the Study of Democratic Institutions, Santa Barbara, Calif. Held in February 1965.

NORTH AMERICAN FEDERATION FOR THE ADVANCEMENT OF PEACE RESEARCH, The Broadmoor, Colorado Springs, Colorado, USA; (Kenneth Boulding, Center for Research on Conflict Resolution, Ann Arbor, Michigan). Held in April 1965.

CIBA FOUNDATION CONFERENCE ON *"Conflict in Society",* Ciba Foundation, 41 Portland Place, London, UK; (A.R.S. de Reuk, Deputy Director, Ciba Foundation, 41 Portland Place, London W I, UK). Held in June 1965.

INTERNATIONAL PEACE RESEARCH INAUGURAL CONFERENCE, Polemological Institute, Groningen, the Netherlands; (B.V.A. Roling, Secretary-General, IPRA, Polemological Institute, Ubbo Emmiussingel 19, Groningen, Netherlands). Held in July 1965.

AMERICAN SOCIOLOGICAL ASSOCIATION Annual Meeting, Chicago, Illinois, on *"Problems of Civilizations and their Changes";* (ASA, Suite 215, 1755 Massachusetts Ave. NW, Washington, DC 20036). Held in August 1965.

INTERNATIONAL CONFERENCE ON THE ECONOMIC OF DISARMAMENT AND CO-EXISTENCE, Oslo, Norway, co-sponsored by RIEDAC (Research on International Economic Effects of Disarmament and Arms Control) and the Peace Research Institute (Oslo); (Peace Research Institute, Oslo, P.O. Box 5052, Oslo, Norway). Held in September 1965.

WORLD PEACE THROUGH WORLD LAW CONFERENCE, Washington DC, USA; a world conference sponsored by the World Peace Through Law Center; (400 Hill Building, Washington, DC). Held in September 1965.

PEACE RESEARCH CONFERENCE, organized by the Peace Research Society (International), somewhere in Central Europe; (Walter Isard, University of Pennsylvania, Philadelphia, Pa.). Held in September 1965.

UNIVERSITY OF LANCASTER, Department of Operational Research, Seminar on "Theoretical Approaches to Conflict"; (H.D. Dunn, Dept. of Operational Research, University of Lancaster, Skein House, 4 Queen's Square, Lancaster, England). Held in October 1965.

MANKIND 2000, first official meeting of sponsors, Ciba Foundation, London; (ICDP, 3 Hendon Ave., London N. 3). Held in November 1965.

NORTH AMERICAN CONFERENCE, PEACE RESEARCH SOCIETY (International), Annenberg School of Communications, University of Pennsylvania, Philadelphia; (Send registrations to W. Isard, Wharton School, U. of Pennsylvania, Philadelphia). Held in November 1965.

WHITE HOUSE CONFERENCE ON an International Cooperation Year Project, (J.A. Amter, Chairman, Committee for Research on the Development of International Institutions, National Citizens Commission on International Cooperation. 2535 First National Bank Building, Denver, Colorado), Held in December 1965.

SIXTH WORLD CONGRESS OF SOCIOLOGY, Evian, France; (P.O. Box 141, Les Acadias, Geneva 24). Held in September 1965.

PEACE RESEARCH CONFERENCE, organized in conjunction with meetings of the Regional Science Association, at the University of Cracow, Cracow, Poland; (direct inquiries to Walter Isard, Peace Research Society (International), University of Pennsylvania, Philadelphia, Pa.). Held in September 1965.

SECOND NORDIC CONFERENCE ON PEACE RESEARCH, Hilleroed, near Copenhagen, Denmark; (A. Boserup, Dronningensgade 1411, Copenhagen K, Denmark). Held in February 1966.

34th UNIVERSAL PEACE CONGRESS, Town-Hall Vincennes, Seine, France; (Congres- Services, I, rue J. Lefebvre, Paris 9, France). Held in April 1966.

SYMPOSIUM ON "CASTE AND RACE: CONFLICT AND ACCOMMODATION IN SOCIETY", London; (Ciba Foundation, 41 Portland Place, London W. I. England, invitational only). Held in April 1966.

INTERNATIONAL STUDIES ASSOCIATION Annual Meeting, Wayne State U., Detroit, Michigan; (Maurice A. Waters, Dept. of Political Science, Wayne State U., Detroit, Mich.). Held in May 1966.

SECOND ACCRA ASSEMBLY, (F. Boaten, P.O. Box 1627, Accra, Ghana). Held in June-July 1966.

PEACE RESEARCH SOCIETY (International) Conference, Institute of Geography, University of Vienna; (R. Gisser, Osterreichisches Institute for Raumplanung. Reichsratsstrasse 17, Vienna). Held in September 1966).

CONFERENCE OF CENTER FOR HUMAN UNDERSTANDING, University of Chicago, "Toward World Community", (J. Nef, 2726 N St. N.W., Washington, D.C.). Held in October 1966.

CONFERENCE ON EDUCATION FOR PEACE (International Institute for Peace, Mollwaldplatz 5, Vienna, Austria). Held in November 1966.

INDEX

A

Alcock, Norman Z., 4, 65
American Friends Service Committee, 122
Anabaptists, the, 68
Angell, Norman, 101
Angell, Robert, 96
Anstey, Edgar, 66
Applied Research, 3ff
Arendt, Hannah, 83
Aron, Raymond, 96
Ayer, Alfred Jules, 21n

B

Bagrit, Leon, 111
Bandung, 55
Bartlett, Ruhl J., 27n
Beaton, Leonard, 111
Bell, R.G., 122
Bernard, Chester, 55
Bernard, Jessie, 96
Birnbaum, Karl, 96
Boasson, Ch., 22n, 63
Bohemian Brethren, 68
Bolshevism, 19
Bondurant, Joan V., 79, 80, 83, 122
Boulding, Kenneth E., 6, 7, 12, 31, 97, 124, 125
Brecht, Arnold, 18
Bridgman, P.W., 22
Britain, 27
British Academy, 3n
Brockway, Fenner A., 27n, 113
Bronowski, Jacob, 19n
Burton, John W., 14, 64

C

Campbell, Norman, 18n
Canada, 27

Carnegie Endowment for International Peace, 100
Carr, E. H., 11n, 42, 43, 101
Carter, April, 113
Case, C.M., 2n, 68, 69, 87
Centre for Research on Conflict Resolution, 12
China, relations with India, 51 ff
Chou En-lai, 54
Christian Pacifism, 36, 71
Ciba Foundation, 99
Clayton, Edward T., 114
Clemens, Walter C., 123
Cohen, Morris R., 21
Collingwood, R.G., 19n
Communist Party, the, 50
Conant, James, 19
Conflict, 6ff; violence and, 96-99
Conflict Studies Movement, 12
Congress Party, the, 49
Cook, Thomas, 10n
Cooper, Peter, 101
Coser, Lewis, 91
Cottrell, W. Fred, 16n, 22n, 63
Cousins, Norman, 94

D

De Crespingy, Anthony, 86, 87
De Kadt, Emanuel, 98
De Light, Bart, 27n,
De Madariaga, Salvador, 101
Deak, Francis, 39
Dellinger, Dave, 88, 89
Demography, 5, 46, 47
Denmark, 39
Deutsch, Karl, 11
Deutsch, Morton, 94n
Dewey, John, 18n
Disarmament, 30; peace research and, 107-112
Diwakar, R.R., 76
Dravida Munnetra Kazhagam, 49, 50
Doukhobors, the, 68
Dunn, Frederick S., 9n
Dunn, Ted, 77, 78, 96, 97

E

Easton, David, 16n
Ebert, Theodor, 121
Eckstein, Harry, 124
Egyptian Passive Resistance, 39
Einstein, Albert, 15
Ellul, Jacques, 111
England, 39
Etzioni, Amitai, 108
Evan, William Mg 94n

F

Fascism, 19
Finland, 39
First World War, 9, 10, 13, 27, 69
Fischer, John, 91
Fisher, R., 97
Fleming, D. F., 99
Food Problem in India, 47 ff
Formosa, 52
Fox, William T. R., 11n
Frank, Jerome D., 95, 118
Frank, Philipp, 23n
France, 27
Friedrich, Carl J., 21n
Fromm, Erich, 83, 92, 94
Fry, Anna Ruth, 27n

G

Galtung, Johan, 9, 28, 63, 64n, 70, 73, 95, 105, 106, 113
Gandhi,
    research on, 35-41
    "influence" on, 38 ff
    "west" and, 38ff
    technique of, 38ff
    relevance of, 38ff
    possibilities of peace research and, 75-90
Gandhi, the Frontier, 40
Gandhian Institute of Studies, 60
Gandhian Pacifism, 36, 70
Gandhian Philosophy, 38
Gee, Wilson, 2n, 23n
General Social Systems Research, 7
Glaser, William A., 16n
Golancz, Victor, 28
Golden, Harry, 115
Good, Charter V., 3n
Goode, William J., 16n
Gotlieb, Allan, 110
Grigg, Charles, 115, 116
Gurian, Waldemar, 9n

H

Hammarskgoeld, Dag, 101
Hammond, Kenneth, 98
Hamon, Leo, 6, 16n, 22n, 64
Hayek, F.A., 18n
Hemleben, S.J., 27n
Hershberger, Guy, 70
Herz, John, 11n
Hocking, W.E., 24, 125
Hoggett, David, 113
Holsti, Ole, 97
Hong Kong, 39
Hrowitz, Irving, 105
Huber, Max, 104
Hudson Institute, the, 12
Hungary,
    nonviolent movement in, 39
Husserl, Edmund, 24
Huxley, Aldous, 25n
Hyneman, Charles S., 5, 19n

I

Ideographic Science, 24
India,
    possibilities of peace research in, 33-61
    fourth general election in, 49
    relations with China, 51ff
    Chinese oggression of, 55
    relations with Pakistan, 56ff
Indian School of International Studies, 60
Indochina, 52
Institute for Social Research, 2n, 16n, 63
Institute for Strategic Studies, 12
International Court of Justice, the, 6, 29
International Police Force, 6
International Relations,
    relationship with peace research, 9-14, 99-107
    realist school of, 11
    systemic school of, 11

J

Janis, Irving, 41
Japan, 27
Japanese Resistance, 39
Jaspers, Karl, 83
Jenkin, Thomas P., 16n
Jones, LeRoi, 73, 74, 75

K

Kahn, Herman, 11
Kant, Immanuel, 27
Kaplan, Morton A., 11
Kashmir, 54, 58, 59
Katz, Daniel, 41
Kaufmann, Felix, 17n
Kennedy, John, 115ff
Khan, Abdul Ghaffar, 40
Khudai Khidmatgar Movement, the, 40, 80
Killian, Lewis, 115, 116
King-Hall, Stephen, 28, 77, 100
King, Martin Luther, 114
Klatt, Paul K., 16n
Klineberg, Otto, 11n, 101
Korean War, 52
Kuper, L., 71

L

Lacombe, Olivier, 88, 89
Lakey, George, 113, 114
Landheer, B., 102
Larson, Arthur, 125
Leach, Edmund, 103
League of Nations, the, 10, 29
Lentz, Theo F., 16n, 22n, 65
Leonard, L., 66
Levi, Werner, 104, 105
Luard, Evan, 107, 110
Lyttle, Bradford, 122

M

MacIver, Robert M., 15
Maddox, John, 111
Madge, John, 17n
Magill, Samuel, 11n
Mahadevan, T.K., 76
Mangone, Gerard J., 27n
Marcuse, Herbert, 126
Maritain, Jacques, 24
Martin, David, 70
Marxism, 82
McClelland, Charles, 11
McNeil, Elton, 91, 99
Mead, Margaret, 125
Melman, Seymour, 108
Mennonites, the, 68
Mill, J.S., 84
Miller, Lynn, 103
Miller, William Robert, 27n, 72, 77
Millis, William, 125
Mills, C. Wright, 28

Moch, Jules, 5, 125
Montgomery Bus Boycott, 39
Moos, Malcolm, 10n
Morgenthau, Hans J., 11n
Morris-Jones, W. H., 76
Morton, Thomas, 94
Moslem Pathans, 40
Mumford, Lewis, 28, 94

N

Naes, Arne, 79, 81, 83, 118
Nagel, Ernest, 3n, 21
Narayan, Jayaprakash, 51, 58, 59
National Socialism, 19
Nazis, 39
Negroes' Resistance, 27
Nehru, 45, 52, 54,, 56
Neo-Gandhians, 34, 35
Nicolson, Harold, 101
Niebuhr, Reinhold, 11n
Nieburg, H. L., 92, 94
Nimbark, Ashakant, 81, 82, 83, 84, 86
Nogee, Joseph, 58
Nomethetic Science, 24
Nonviolence,
    peace research and, 67-75
Nonviolent Civil Defence, 116-26
North, Robert, 97
Northrop, F.S.C., 17n
North West Frontier Province, 40
Norway, 27, 34, 39
Norwegian Teachers' Resistance, 39
Nunn, A.C., 112

O

Oppenheimer, Martin, 67, 91n, 114
Osgood, Charles, 58

P

Pakistan,
    relations with India, 56ff
Passive Resistance,
    distinction between peace research and, 27ff
Pauling, Linus, 79
Paullin, Theodor, 71
Peace,
    meaning of, 2, 5ff
    one-factor theories of, 28, 30
    as integrated behaviour, 43ff
    conceptual growth of, 4
    warlessness as, 6

Peace Movement, 34
  distinction between peace research and, 26ff
Peace Research,
  definition of, 1, 2, 3, 14, 22, 63-67
  as an independent science, 14ff 22, 24, 29, 30, 31, 32, 33
  social sciences and, 7ff, 23-24, 29
  as a philosophical science, 24
  as a scientific philosophy, 24
  two stages of the development of, 25
  as a *master discipline* and *umbrella science*, 25
  pure sciences and, 25
  national policies and, 25-26
  peace movement and, 26-32
  the present state of, 1-32
  national and international peace research, 33, 34
  scope of, 7ff
  as a value science, 17ff
  nonviolence and, 67-75
  violence and, 90-96
  international relations and, 99-107
  disarmament and arms control and, 107-112
  population control and, 47ff
  food problem and, 47ff
Peaceful Resistance,
  technique of, 112-116
Pear, T. H., 96
Penrose, Margaret, 123
Philosophy,
  meaning of, 15ff
Polemologische Institute, 12
Pontara, Giuliamo, 70n, 89, 90
Population Problem in India, 46-48
Power, Paul F., 76, 77, 78
Porterfield, Arthur L., 91
Propaganda,
  peace research and, 30ff
Pure Research, 4ff

Q

Quakers, 2, 28, 68
Quisling Regime, 39

R

Rajagopalachari, Chakravarti, 51
Ramachandran, G., 76
Rand Corporation, the, 12
Rapoport, Anatol, 11, 58, 107
Read, Herbert, 93, 94
Red Cross, 29

Reichenbach, Hans, 20n
Research, meaning of, 2, 3, 4ff
Reynolds, Reginald, 70
Richardson, Lewis, 11, 109
Robert, Adam, 113, 118
Roling, B. V. A., 64
Rosecrance, R. N., 109
Rosenau, James, 11n
Rudolph, Susanne Hoeber, 87, 88
Ruge, Mari Holmboe, 106
Ruhr, the, 39
Ruskin, 38
Russell, Bertrand, 28, 82
Russell, Frank, 2n, 27n

S

Sabine, George, 16n
Scates, Douglas E., 3n
Schelling, Thomas, 11, 58
Science,
  meaning of, 15ff
Science of Peace, 16
Scientific Method, the, 17 ff
Second World War, 13, 19, 27
Security Council, 6
Sharp, Gene, 27n, 71-72, 77, 83, 97 113, 117, 118
Sheean, Vincent, 83
Shotwell, James, 101
Sibley, Mulford Q., 71, 123
Sinai, I. R., 124
Singer, J. David, 107
Smith, David G., 24
Smoker, Paul, 108
Sohn, Louis, 125
South African Defy Unjust Laws Campaign, 39
Soviet Union, the, 39
Spits, F. C., 103
Stein, Walter, 94
Stone, Julius, 33
Suhrawardy, H. S., 54
Sunakawa, 39
Swatantra Party, the, 50
Sweden, 34, 39

T

Taiwan, 52
Tanter, Raymond, 99
Technological Engineering Research, 7
Theory,
  meaning of, 16 ff
Thompson, Kenneth W., 9n, 11n
Thoreau, 38

Tibet, 52
Tinker, Hugh, 84, 85, 86
Tolstoy, 38
Toma, Peter A., 9n
Toynbee, Arnold J., 79, 125
Transarmament, 117
Transition Research, 7
Tucker, Robert W., 104

U

Unesco, 2, 96
Unilateralism, 28 ff
United Nations, the, 2, 29, 48, 52, 54, 104
United States, the, 28, 34, 39
Unity of Science, concept of, 23
University of Michigan, 12
University of Mysore, 61
Unnithan, T. K. N., 91n

V

Van Dyke, Vernon, 17
Van Heek, F., 105
Van Slyck, Philip, 102
Veblen, Thorstein, 25n
Viet Minh, 52
Violence,
  peace research and, 90-95
  conflict and, 96-99
  legitimate use of, 45 ff
Vipont, Elfrida, 2n

Voegelin, Eric, 24
Vorkuta Prison Camp, 39

W

Wadsworth, James, 125
Walter, E.V., 92
Waskow, Arthur, 67, 98, 102
Weaver, Anthony, 97
Weber, Max, 3n, 82
Webster, C. K., 27n
Weinberg, A., 97
Weinberg, L., 97
West Samoa, 39
Whitehead, A. N., 20
Wight, Martin, 11n
Williamson, Robert C., 94
Wolf, A., 23
Wolfenstein, E. Victor, 123
Wooton, Barbara, 17n
World Decentralization, 28
World Government, 28, 30
World Law, 28
Wright, Quincy, 11, 63, 94n, 103

Y

Young, Roland, 21n

Z

Zahn, Gordon, 122

Augsburg College
George Sverdrup Library
Minneapolis, Minnesota 55404